KNOCK ME A KISS

by
CHARLES SMITH

Dramatic Publishing
Woodstock, Illinois • England • Australia • New Zealand

IMPORTANT BILLING AND CREDIT REQUIREMENTS

On April 9, 1928, Countee Cullen was married to Yolande Du Bois, the daughter of W.E.B. Du Bois. The Reverend Cullen, Countee's father, officiated over the wedding which W.E.B. Du Bois called "the symbolic march of young and black America...it was a new race, a new thought, a new thing rejoicing in a ceremony as old as the world."

Two months later, Countee Cullen sailed to Paris with the best man from the wedding, Harold Jackman, leaving Yolande, his young bride, behind. Yolande was granted a divorce from Countee on December 9, 1929.

This play is a fictional account inspired by those factual events.

Knock Me a Kiss was originally produced by Victory Gardens Theater (Dennis Zacek, artistic director; Marcelle McVay, managing director) in Chicago, Illionis, on January 21, 2000. It was directed by Chuck Smith; the set design was by Mary Griswold; the costume design was by Birgit Rattenborg Wise; the lighting design was by Todd Hensley; the sound design was by Benjamin T. Getting and Benjamin Recht; the production stage manager was Tina M. Jack. The cast was as follows:

Jimmy Luncefore	MOROCCO OMARI
Yolande Du Bois	YVONNE HUFF
Nina Du Bois	CELESTE WILLIAMS
W.E.B. Du Bois	DEXTER ZOLLICOFFER
Countee Cullen	JASON DELANE
Lenora	LESHAY TOMLINSON

KNOCK ME A KISS

A Play in Two Acts
For 3 Men and 3 Women

CHARACTERS

YOLANDE DU BOIS: The 26-year-old daughter of
W.E.B. Du Bois and Nina Du Bois. Yolande is a romantic who has led a very sheltered life. The greatest love
she has in her life is the love she has for her father.

JIMMY LUNCEFORD: A 28-year-old big band leader.
Graduate of Fisk University and former high school
teacher, Jimmy decided that the hand-to-mouth existence
of touring on the road with a band he formed was more
important to him than maintaining a steady job teaching
high school. He is down to earth and very practical, up
on current trends and fashions and meticulous when it
comes to music. He has a good business sense and loves
Yolande dearly.

NINA DU BOIS: In her mid-60s, she is the wife of W.E.B.
Du Bois. Nina has a very provincial attitude toward sex
which she considers to be fundamentally dirty but necessary. She lives in the shadow of her husband whom she
met when he was a professor and she was a student taking one of his classes. The death of her son Burghardt at
18 months, a death from which she never fully recov-
ered, was fundamental in forming her attitude toward her
daughter, Yolande, who was born later, and toward her

husband, W.E.B., whom she considered responsible for Burghardt's death.

WILLIAM EDWARD BURGHARDT (W.E.B.) DU BOIS: Mid-60s, but very young for his age. Active in national and international politics, he has come to recognize that he is a better politician than he is a husband and father. Even so, he considers his personal sacrifices for the promotion of his personal agenda well worth it. He maintains a very businesslike relationship with his wife and his daughter.

COUNTEE CULLEN: A 25-year-old boy-poet genius and protégé of W.E.B. Du Bois, he is clearly a product of the Ivory Tower, Talented Tenth machine. He is very warm and charming, a man who has used words to get into and out of any situation.

LENORA: Friend and confidant of Yolande, she's the down-to-earth, no-nonsense, tell-it-like-it-is-type of friend we all would like to have.

SET: The set should consist of four or five acting areas. Together, the first three acting areas should constitute the Du Bois apartment on West 150th Street in Harlem. These areas include the foyer outside of the front door to the apartment, a common area inside the apartment, and the book-laden study of W.E.B. Du Bois. The other areas, Jimmy Lunceford's rehearsal hall and Countee Cullen's apartment, should only be suggested.

TIME: 1928.

PLACE: Harlem.

ACT ONE

Scene One

The Du Bois apartment. YOLANDE enters into the foyer outside of the front door to the apartment. She is followed by JIMMY Lunceford. The hour is late—somewhere between one and two in the morning. As they enter, JIMMY sings. YOLANDE tries to quiet him as she fumbles with her keys.

JIMMY. I like cake and no mistake
     But baby if you insist…
YOLANDE. Shhh!
JIMMY. I'll cut out cake
     Just for your sake…
YOLANDE. Quiet!

(He stops singing.)

JIMMY. Baby, we was swanging.
YOLANDE. If you're gonna come in here, you're gonna have to be quiet.
JIMMY. Am I right?
YOLANDE. Jimmy…
JIMMY. Just tell me. Was we swanging or what?
YOLANDE. All right. You were swinging.

JIMMY. Swinging? No, uh-uh, baby, we wasn't swinging. The Duke, he be swinging. Cab Calloway was swinging. But us, baby, we was swanging.

YOLANDE. I didn't know there was a difference.

JIMMY. You know what the difference is. When you swinging, you only going through the motions, you doing it how you think it should be done, you only repeating what you've heard. But when you swanging, baby, the motions are going through you, you making it up as you go along, you are following a voice that's coming to you from somewhere deep down inside.

(YOLANDE gets the door open as they enter the apartment.)

YOLANDE. You're gonna have to be quiet, Jimmy.

JIMMY. Ain't nobody home.

YOLANDE. My father isn't home. My mother, she's always here. She never goes anyplace.

JIMMY. Exactly what I expected.

YOLANDE. Is that right?

JIMMY. Yes sir. This here is one swank stack of bricks.

YOLANDE. Swank?

JIMMY. That's right. I expected your old man to live in a joint like this. Books. Very intellectual. All in the head, you see. Nothing in the heart.

YOLANDE. How you know?

JIMMY. I know your ole man.

YOLANDE. I didn't realize you two were such aces.

JIMMY. Don't have to be his boon coon. Don't even have to meet the man. Listen to you talk about him all the time. Talk about how you used to sit here waiting for him to come home.

YOLANDE. You want your drink or not?

JIMMY. I'd rather get a lil taste of something else.

YOLANDE. I swear to God you got a one-track mind.

JIMMY. Ain't my fault you put a conjure on me. Every time I close my eyes, all I can see is you. Your eyes, your lips sweet like candy, peaches and bananas, like a couple of Louisiana plums.

YOLANDE. Jimmy...

JIMMY. Come here and let me run my tongue across those sweet plums of yours.

YOLANDE. Please.

JIMMY. Come on and knock me a kiss.

YOLANDE. My mother's here.

JIMMY. I'll be quiet. I swear. Quieter than a mouse pissing on cotton.

YOLANDE. How many times I have to tell you?

JIMMY. And I won't go too far. When you want me to stop, I'll stop. Promise.

YOLANDE. I'm not fooling around with you. Especially not here.

JIMMY. Then come back with me to my place, Yolande. Come on.

YOLANDE. I'm not going back to that rattrap you call a room.

JIMMY. Well I'm sorry, but we all can't afford to stay at the Waldorf.

YOLANDE. Maybe not.

JIMMY. We ain't all connected like you.

YOLANDE. Don't have to be connected to afford to stay someplace better than you staying now.

JIMMY. Okay. Tell you what I'm gonna do. If it's that important to you, snatch up your stuff and let's go down to that swank stack on the boulevard and get ourselves a real nice room. A suite, order a bottle of bubbles, something to eat…

YOLANDE. You can't even afford a decent room. How you gonna afford a bottle of bubbles?

JIMMY. I got kick.

YOLANDE. Since when?

JIMMY. Since the hen broke wind. Check it out. *(He produces an envelope which contains a stack of bills. He fans the money out and begins to count it.)* Ten, twenty, thirty…

YOLANDE. Where'd you get that?

JIMMY. Forty, sixty, eighty, one hundred.

(There is more.)

YOLANDE. Jimmy…

JIMMY. As you can see, I can obviously afford to purchase a bottle of bubbles.

YOLANDE. That's the band's money, ain't it?

JIMMY. My money.

YOLANDE. You better not be messing with them men's money.

JIMMY. Who's the head nigger in charge? I'm the head nigger in charge.

YOLANDE. Why you always have to use that word?

JIMMY. What word?

YOLANDE. You know what word.

JIMMY. Nigger?

YOLANDE. That word.

JIMMY. Hell, it's true. I am the head nigger in charge. It is my band, I'm the HNIC, and I say, if you want a nice room, you want a lil champagne, we go get ourselves a sweet suite and a bottle of bubbles. Nothin' but the best for my baby.

YOLANDE. Do I look like I just got off the boat?

JIMMY. What boat?

YOLANDE. You think that all you have to do is rent a room and buy a bottle of booze to have your way with me?

JIMMY. I'm trying to give you want you want.

YOLANDE. What I want is to get married, Jimmy.

JIMMY. Okay. Let's get married.

YOLANDE. When?

JIMMY. Name the time and the place.

YOLANDE. How 'bout here and how 'bout now?

JIMMY. Unless you got a preacher in your pocket, baby, we gonna least have to wait till the morning. So how about this? Tonight, we get ourselves a nice room and get real comfortable. Let me curl your toes a lil bit, you curl mine. Then, first thing in the morning, we'll go down to city hall and jump us some broom. What you think about that?

YOLANDE. Was that supposed to be a marriage proposal?

JIMMY. All right. I can see where this is going. Yolande, will you marry me?

YOLANDE. No one will ever accuse you of being a Valentino.

JIMMY. You said you wanted to get married.

YOLANDE. You make it sound like I asked you to clean out my bathtub drain.

JIMMY. I said I'd do it. Damn.

YOLANDE. I want to get married with a little romance, Jimmy. I don't want to get married by no judge. Judges shouldn't be marrying people. Judges send people to jail.

JIMMY. Don't matter who says the words. Long as we believe them.

YOLANDE. We get married tomorrow, where we gonna go on our honeymoon?

JIMMY. Dayton.

YOLANDE. Dayton?

JIMMY. Dayton, Ohio. Got a gig at a stomp shop there Friday next. We get married, get on the bus, go to Dayton and indulge ourselves in some sweet honeymoon.

YOLANDE. Is that all you ever think about?

JIMMY. My lips and your plums on our honeymoon.

YOLANDE. Jimmy...

JIMMY. I'm a man, baby. Shit, if I wasn't thinking about it, something be wrong.

YOLANDE. All right. I want you to do something for me.

JIMMY. You know I'll do any damn thing for you.

(YOLANDE hands a silver-tipped walking cane to JIMMY.)

YOLANDE. Here.

JIMMY. What's this?

YOLANDE. What's it look like?

JIMMY. Looks like a cane but I ain't gimpy. Nothing wrong with my legs.

YOLANDE. It's not that type of cane, Jimmy. Here. Take it. Stand over here.

JIMMY. For what?

YOLANDE. I wanna see what you look like.

JIMMY. Don't you already know what I look like?

YOLANDE. Jimmy!

JIMMY. All right. *(JIMMY takes the cane and moves to the bookcases.)*

YOLANDE. Stand up straight. Come on. Hold your chin up, Jimmy. When was the last time you talked to your mother and father?

JIMMY. My mother and father?

YOLANDE. The people who gave birth to you?

JIMMY. This is your daddy's cane, ain't it?

YOLANDE. It's nobody's cane.

JIMMY. You trying to make me look like your daddy.

YOLANDE. I'm trying to imagine what you gonna look like at the wedding.

JIMMY. I can tell you this: Whatever I look like, I'm not gonna be carrying your daddy's silver-tipped walking stick. I can tell you that.

YOLANDE. And I'm not getting on a bus and going to Dayton, Ohio, for a honeymoon with you. When I get married, I wanna get married in a church, Jimmy. With flowers and a ring.

JIMMY. What kinda ring?

YOLANDE. Diamond ring. I want a diamond engagement ring and I want a wedding ring. I want a church wedding with lotsa flowers and ushers and bridesmaids. And on my honeymoon, I wanna sail on a boat, Jimmy, first class. I wanna sail to Paris or Vienna. I'm not getting on nobody's bus going to no damn Dayton, Ohio.

JIMMY. You want a society wedding.

YOLANDE. I want a wedding that corresponds to my stature. According to who I am.

JIMMY. You are sounding more and more like your daddy every day.

YOLANDE. And what's wrong with that?

JIMMY. Nothing, if you don't mind sounding saddity.

YOLANDE. Saddity?

JIMMY. Your daddy is one of the most sadditiest Negroes I've ever seen in my life. Saddity and self-righteous, that man's nose so high up in the air, if it rained, he'd drown. And now here you come, you starting to act just like him.

YOLANDE. I'm about tired of you passing judgment on my father.

JIMMY. I don't care nothing about your daddy. Hell, he don't care nothing about me. I don't fit into his master plan of producing a batch of upper-crust Negroes. Shit, what I care about him for? And I'll tell you something else: I ain't scared of him either. Everybody walking around this country scared of that nigger. I ain't scared of him and I don't care who knows it. In fact, I can't wait till I meet him. Hell, I'll tell him to his face exactly what I think of him. Shit, the way I see it, he's just like every other nigger walking the face of this earth. He's just as—

YOLANDE. That's enough, Jimmy.

JIMMY. I'm sorry, Yolande, but I got to call it like I see it.

YOLANDE. And now I'm gonna call it like I see it. If you ever wrap your mouth around my father or his reputation again, I swear to God, Jimmy Lunceford, I will break it off with you so hard, fast and complete I won't even leave a memory behind. You understand me?

JIMMY. All I'm saying is, your daddy—

YOLANDE. I know what you saying and I'm tired of hearing it. My father has worked too long and too hard to
have some ignorant son of a Negro like you come along
and badmouth him.

JIMMY. So why I got to be ignorant?

YOLANDE. Call it like I see it.

JIMMY. Let me say something before we start to drift too
far from land. I love you, Yolande, and I will marry you
any day, any time, all you have to do is say the word.
However, I can't afford no diamond rangs and no church
weddings and no honeymoons in Vienna. At least not
now. I'm struggling right now, baby. If somethin' comes
outta tonight, if that cat from the Cotton Club dug us or
if that cat from the Lafayette liked what he heard, if either one of 'em books us for a gig here in Harlem, baby,
we'll be picking in high cotton. Hell, we just as good as
the Duke. We just as good if not better than Cab
Calloway. I mean, what the hell is hi-de hi-de ho? Don't
nobody know. People sing it, but they don't know what
the hell they singing. So why did Cab Calloway come
up with it? 'Cause it distinguishes him and his band
from everybody else and they band. And that's all I got
to do. Distinguish me and my band from everybody else.
Soon as I figure out a way. to do that, I guarantee you,
we'll be playing all over this town, and maybe then, I'll
have enough money for diamonds and church weddings.
But until that happens, I got to keep on playing Dayton,
and Cincinnati and Buffalo and every little gut-bucket in
between. You wanna come along? Baby, you're certainly welcome.

YOLANDE. I'm not traveling with you as your concubine.

JIMMY. I already told ya I'd marry ya.

YOLANDE. You just don't understand romance, do you?

JIMMY. I guess that's just something I'm just gonna have to work on. You wanna go back to my place with me or not?

YOLANDE. What did I tell ya?

JIMMY. Can I at least have a good-night kiss?

(She acquiesces. He kisses her. She kisses him. After a moment, his hands develop a mind of their own.)

YOLANDE. Jimmy… *(He continues.)* Please don't touch me there. *(He likes it.)* Jimmy!

JIMMY. All right. Sorry. Sleep tight, Honeymoon.

(JIMMY exits. NINA, who was eavesdropping on the scene, enters.)

YOLANDE. Jesus. Must you always spy on me.

NINA. Must you always use that type of language?

YOLANDE. You'd think a woman could have a little privacy.

NINA. A woman doesn't need privacy. Not a proper woman. The only type of woman that needs privacy is a woman who's doing something she's not supposed to be doing. But then, you wouldn't call that type of woman a woman, now would you?

YOLANDE. I wasn't doing anything improper.

NINA. I heard a man's voice.

YOLANDE. That was Jimmy.

NINA. He's a man.

YOLANDE. I wasn't doing anything, Mother.

NINA. Two o'clock in the morning.

YOLANDE. He walked me home.

NINA. Man, woman, two o'clock in the morning.

YOLANDE. So what? If I stayed out until five o'clock in the morning, what's it to you?

NINA. Doesn't mean anything to me. Might mean something to your father, though.

YOLANDE. I haven't done anything wrong.

NINA. Didn't say you did. Just saying that your father might be interested in knowing about this behavior.

YOLANDE. Jimmy is a friend of mine, Mother.

NINA. A friend?

YOLANDE. That's all. There is no behavior.

NINA. You've been out with your friend almost every night this week.

YOLANDE. I am twenty-six years old. I should be able to go out with whomever I please.

NINA. We'll see what your father has to say about that.

YOLANDE. Tell him. I don't care. You think I live my life to please Daddy? Is that what you think? I don't care what you tell him. I'm not gonna be here when he gets here anyway.

NINA. And where do you think you're going?

YOLANDE. Daddy's not here, I'm going back to Baltimore.

NINA. Why do you have to keep an apartment in Baltimore, Yolande? What's wrong with living here in New York?

YOLANDE. I plan to begin my work in Baltimore, Mother.

NINA. What work?

YOLANDE. I plan to follow in Daddy's footsteps and dedicate my life to the betterment of the Negro race.

NINA. And somebody told you that Baltimore was the place to go if you wanted to begin this betterment?

YOLANDE. I plan to teach high school in Baltimore, Mother.

NINA. High school?

YOLANDE. I plan to help the downtrodden and the less fortunate.

NINA. That's like the blind leading the blind. You're just as downtrodden and are at least as less fortunate as everybody else.

YOLANDE. I'm not gonna allow you to depress me.

NINA. You should forget about helping others and think about helping yourself, Yolande.

YOLANDE. They want me, Mother. They need me. They asked me to come in for an interview at three o'clock tomorrow afternoon.

NINA. Then you will miss seeing your father because he'll be here tomorrow morning.

YOLANDE. Tomorrow morning?

NINA. The 10:45 from Pittsburgh.

YOLANDE. Why didn't you say something?

NINA. You weren't here to say something to.

YOLANDE. Look at me. I have to to the beauty shop. I have to get my hair done. And look at this dress. Mother, you should have said something. I have to go shopping. There's not enough time.

NINA. Doesn't matter what you look like once your father finds out that you've been carrying on with that musician.

YOLANDE. I haven't been carrying on.

NINA. We'll let your father be the judge of that.

Scene Two

The next morning. COUNTEE Cullen and W.E.B. Du Bois in the Du Bois study.

COUNTEE. I turned in the application. They sent me a letter, we set up an appointment, I went in and met with them. Everything is exactly how it should be. They asked about you, how you felt about it. I told them that I'd talk to you.

WILL. What do they want?

COUNTEE. I think what they want is some sort of acknowledgment.

WILL. From me?

COUNTEE. Something simple. A good word, a note perhaps.

WILL. You mean a recommendation.

COUNTEE. I've been after this for the past six years, Dr. Du Bois. If I get this award, I'd be able to study abroad for at least a year if not two. I'll be able to walk in the footsteps of Shelley and Keats.

WILL. And what about your brethren here at home, Countee? Tell me how you walking in the footsteps of dead European poets would benefit the Negro of the United States?

COUNTEE. You mean besides the obvious contribution to my personal growth as a poet?

WILL. It's time for you to look beyond your personal growth. It's time for you to take into consideration the impact of your actions upon the lives of others. You're in the public eye. You're a Negro and you're a poet. Like it or not, everything you do from here on in will have meaning. Every action you take will be dismantled,

examined and interpreted, then reassembled and reinter-
preted.

COUNTEE. I am aware of the glare of public scrutiny.

WILL. Are you?

COUNTEE. Well aware.

WILL. Then why haven't you married?

COUNTEE. Is that necessary?

WILL. We've spent a great deal of time and energy extol-
ling the virtues of marriage, the value of family, the im-
portance of black love within the family. And here you
are, in your late twenties, a highly visible vanguard of
the struggle and you are, as of yet, unmarried. No matter
how you turn it, it doesn't look good, Countee. It makes
it appear as if we don't practice what we preach. Now
you know that I support you and your work. But if you
want me to give you something more, an acknowledgment, a good word, a note perhaps, you're gonna have to
help me. Help me help you.

COUNTEE. By taking a wife?

WILL. There must be a host of eligible young women who
have caught your eye. Simply choose one.

COUNTEE. How?

WILL. What do you mean, how?

COUNTEE. How do I choose?

WILL. Examine blood lines. Heredity, physique, health and
brains. Make sure you avoid putting emphasis on beauty
or something as fleeting as romantic sexual allure.

COUNTEE. I understand all of this, Dr. Du Bois.

WILL. Then I don't understand your question.

COUNTEE. I'm not sure how to begin.

WILL. Do as I did. Get a piece of paper and make three
columns. In the first column, list the names of all of the

eligible young women you know. In the next column, list the attributes of each woman, and in the last column, list their shortcomings. Subtract the shortcomings of each woman from her attributes and the woman with the most attributes, you choose as your wife.

COUNTEE. Sounds a bit impersonal to me.

WILL. Systematic is what it is, my boy. Too often we are ruled by our emotions. We make irrational decisions based on something silly as love or momentary desire. Love is familiarity. Nothing more, nothing less. For instance, the town I lived in as a child was home to a slaughterhouse. Every week hundreds of hogs were butchered, hung, bled and dressed for the market. The smell of blood and carnage permeated the entire town. Strangers who would come to town would cover their mouth and nose. They'd always ask the same question: "What's that God-awful smell?" And our reply to that question was always the same. "That smell, my friend, is the smell of money." After the slaughterhouse closed, the entire town went into mourning. We mourned not only the loss of the economic river that dried up after the slaughterhouse closed, but we mourned the loss of the slaughterhouse itself, the activity, the sounds, the sight of it all lit up at night churning out waxed boxes of hams, bacon, pork chops and steaks. But most of all, we mourned the loss of the smell. It was part of our prosperity, part of who we were. Now, if an entire town can grow to love the smell of spilt blood, carnage and death, I imagine it wouldn't be difficult for one man to grow to love a woman who he chose after careful deliberation. That's how I chose Nina. We've been married now for thirty-two happy years.

COUNTEE. Okay. Make a list.

WILL. And then choose.

COUNTEE. After I choose?

WILL. After you choose, ask your potential wife out on a date. This should be a real date, Countee, don't invite her to a poetry reading or recital. Friends, you invite to hear your poetry. A potential wife, you invite out for an evening of dinner. But not dancing. You don't want her to get the wrong idea. Dancing is permitted only after the second or third date. And make sure you buy her some flowers. Women like that sort of thing. Flowers.

COUNTEE. Flowers?

WILL. Didn't your father teach you any of this?

COUNTEE. My father doesn't understand me.

WILL. I'm sure he does.

COUNTEE. Not the way you do.

(YOLANDE enters.)

YOLANDE. Daddy's home! Daddy! Surprise!

WILL. Ouchie!

YOLANDE *(hugs him)*. Surprised?

WILL. Surprised and happy. I thought you were to be in Baltimore.

YOLANDE. I was but I came in last week to be here to surprise you when you got home, but Mother wouldn't tell me when you were coming. First she said you were gonna be here Friday, then she said it was gonna be another week so I decided I was gonna go back to Baltimore for a job interview but last night she told me you were coming home today which didn't leave me with enough time to go shopping or get my hair done 'cause I couldn't get an appointment on such short notice and that's the reason my hair looks the way it does. Hey, Countee.

COUNTEE. Hey.

WILL. Your hair looks fine, Ouchie. I like it like this. It's a new look for you.

YOLANDE. The unpressed look?

WILL. It must be your inner splendor that I see shining through. Now what's this about a job interview?

YOLANDE. I'm gonna teach high school, Daddy. In Baltimore. I'm gonna work with the less fortunate.

WILL. Good girl. That's my girl. You hear this, Countee? Yolande is joining the struggle.

(NINA enters.)

NINA. Will? I must talk to you about your daughter's behavior.

YOLANDE. Here she goes.

NINA. She's been out with a man every night this week.

YOLANDE. I've already told you that he's just a friend of mine.

NINA. He keeps her out until two, three o'clock in the morning.

YOLANDE. Nobody keeps me out, Mother.

NINA. He must be the one keeping you out because I know you do not stay out till the wee hours of the morning on your own.

YOLANDE. I am a grown woman.

COUNTEE. I oughta be going.

WILL. Wait, Countee, please.

YOLANDE. I am fully capable of making responsible choices on my own.

WILL. Ouchie? Is this true?

YOLANDE. Is what true, Daddy?

WILL. Has my little girl met a young man?

NINA. What did I just tell you? I just told you, she's been out with him every night this week.

WILL. Wife, please.

NINA. Am I making words here? Can anyone hear me?

WILL. Yolande?

YOLANDE. He's a friend, Daddy. That's all.

NINA. We know nothing about this man. We know nothing about his background, nothing about his breeding or his upbringing.

YOLANDE. He graduated from Fisk, Mother.

NINA. What about his parents? What do we know about them? And his parents' parents?

YOLANDE. You just eliminated half of all the eligible Negro bachelors in Harlem.

WILL. Ouchie? This friend of yours. What's his name?

YOLANDE. Jimmy Lunceford.

WILL. Is he someone I should meet?

YOLANDE. No, Daddy. There's no need.

NINA. He's a musician.

WILL. Nevertheless, Wife, we could invite him to dinner. Him and his parents. We could get to know his family, discover what type of young man he is.

YOLANDE. I'm telling ya, Daddy, he's just a friend. Somebody I met through Lenora.

WILL. If he's someone you're seeing, I would like to meet him, Yolande.

YOLANDE. The only reason I went out with him in the first place was because I was bored. There's nothing for me to do here in New York or in Baltimore. For example, I would love to go out with a man like Countee...

WILL. Countee?

YOLANDE. However, Countee has not asked me out on a date. And if he doesn't ask me out on a date, I can't go out with him, now can I?

WILL. Well I'm sure if Countee knew you were interested...

NINA. Excuse me, but I hardly think it appropriate to talk about the young man as if he weren't even here.

COUNTEE. I could leave.

WILL. No, wait, Countee.

YOLANDE. There's a dearth of eligible Negro bachelors in this country. Especially well-traveled, well-bred, sophisticated ones. A man like Countee is exactly the type of man I've been looking for.

NINA. She is shameless.

WILL. Wife, please.

YOLANDE. Thank you, Daddy. At least somebody around here treats me with respect.

NINA. Are you encouraging this type of behavior?

WILL. I think the children need to work this out for themselves.

YOLANDE. We're not children.

WILL. You're right, I'm sorry, you're not.

YOLANDE. We are both mature and responsible adults.

WILL. Capable of making responsible choices on your own, I know. Countee?

COUNTEE. Would you like to have dinner with me, Yolande?

YOLANDE. I would love to have dinner with you, Countee.
NINA. Shameless. She is absolutely shameless.

Scene Three

Few days later. YOLANDE is getting dressed. LENORA is helping her with her hair.

LENORA. So I go by the rehearsal hall but I don't hear no music. I figure they either taking a break or ain't nobody there. I walk in and find out that everybody's there and they ain't taking no break, they're practicing. But they ain't practicing no music. Get this...they're practicing their walk.
YOLANDE. Their walk?
LENORA. Jimmy got everybody on one side of the room, teaching them how to walk to the other side of the room.
YOLANDE. They're grown men. Don't they already know how to walk?
LENORA. Not the way Jimmy teaching them how to walk. Jimmy teaching them how to strut. All together, in step. He's calls it synchronized syncopation.
YOLANDE. He's converting his band to a marching band?
LENORA. I ain't seen them play music when they walk. He got them strutting in step when they walk on stage before they start playing and strutting in step when they walk off stage after they get done playing. He also got them swanging they horns and nodding they heads and waving they hands all together, all while playing.
YOLANDE. Negro's lost his mind.

LENORA. Lost his mind over you is what happened. He told me he asked you to marry him.

YOLANDE. Is that right?

LENORA. That's what he said. S'it true?

YOLANDE. If you wanna call it that.

LENORA. He asked you to marry him?

YOLANDE. He only asked me 'cause he thought I wanted him to ask me.

LENORA. You didn't want him to ask?

YOLANDE. Not the way he did. He didn't mean it. He didn't get down on one knee, he didn't have a ring, he didn't talk to my father and he's gonna have to talk to my father.

LENORA. You need permission to get married?

YOLANDE. I don't need no permission.

LENORA. Then why he gotta talk to your father?

YOLANDE. It's a show of respect, Lenora, to ask the father for a woman's hand in marriage. He wouldn't be asking for my father's permission, he'd be asking for his blessing.

LENORA. I can't see Jimmy asking no man for nothing.

YOLANDE. See what I'm saying? I can't take him seriously 'cause he really didn't mean it.

LENORA. Wouldn't matter to me. Soon as those words fell from his lips, I'd snatch them up and hold him to it. I'd worry about whether he meant it later, after the wedding. Shoot. There are plenty of ways of making a man mean it. Long list of ways. The trick is to get him to stay in one place long enough to work some of them ways on him. Get him to sit still, hell, I'll make him mean it.

YOLANDE. Which color? *(She holds up a couple tubes of lipstick.)*

LENORA. Ain't you going out on a date?

YOLANDE. Right.

LENORA. So why you asking me? Wear the red, baby. Rhythm red. You know what I mean?

YOLANDE. I'm going out with the son of a preacher.

LENORA. You talking about Countee?

YOLANDE. I ain't talking about Jimmy.

LENORA. Countee Cullen is not the son of a preacher.

YOLANDE. His daddy is a reverend, Lenora. Got a church on 125th Street.

LENORA. That man is not his daddy. Not the way I heard it.

YOLANDE. No telling what you heard, the people you hang out with.

LENORA. What's that supposed to mean?

YOLANDE. I've known Countee for six years.

LENORA. I don't care how long you've known him. I'm just telling you what I heard. You don't wanna hear it, just say so. You ain't hurt my feelings 'cause it don't matter to me.

YOLANDE. All right. Let's hear it.

LENORA. I don't wanna be guilty of foisting upon you any rumor, innuendo, through your window or out your window. I'll keep my little bit of information to myself.

YOLANDE. You want me to beg you?

LENORA. Crawling on your hands and knees.

YOLANDE. I'm not gonna beg you.

LENORA. All right. The way I heard it, Countee Cullen was an orphan. Reverend Cullen and his wife took the boy in when the boy was about fifteen, sixteen years old.

YOLANDE. This is the first I've ever heard of this lie.

LENORA. Everybody been talking about it for years. It was real interesting 'cause the Reverend and his wife couldn't have no kids. Most folks say that it was because of the wife, that she had narrow hips. But other folks say it was because of the Reverend. That he was a bit peculiar, you know what I'm saying? The Reverend was peculiar and then here he shows up with a fifteen-year-old boy that he claimed to be his son.

YOLANDE. I ain't never heard of this before.

LENORA. There's a whole lot out there that you ain't never heard of before.

YOLANDE. My father knows his father, Lenora.

LENORA. You not hearing about it don't make it not true.

YOLANDE. They've been friends for as long as I can remember. If that was true, I'd know about it.

LENORA. Why you going out with him for anyway?

YOLANDE. I like him. He's a poet.

LENORA. Jimmy's a poet. And he find out you going out with this man, he really gonna lose his mind.

YOLANDE. Don't nobody care about Jimmy.

LENORA. When all this change?

YOLANDE. Every time he comes to town he's staying in another nasty room. I don't like those places he stay in. Makes my skin crawl.

LENORA. Not his fault he's a broke Negro.

YOLANDE. I'm tired of him putting his hands all over me every time I see him.

LENORA. Let him put them paws on me. I wouldn't complain.

YOLANDE. Every time I see him, he's got only one thing on his mind.

LENORA. Wouldn't complain one bit.

YOLANDE. I want a little romance and all he can think about is sex.

LENORA. What's the difference?

YOLANDE. Romance is tender kisses and caressing in the moonlight. And sex is…sex. It's dark and it's groping and poking and although won't nobody admit it, it's a bit scary.

LENORA. I don't know what kind of sex you having but sound like you doing something wrong.

YOLANDE. I want him to bring me some flowers every now and then. What's wrong with that? What's wrong with me expecting him to dust off a few sweet words to say to me instead of talking about his music all the time? You know what I would like? I would like to spend an evening with him without him trying to hop on top of me at the end of that evening. Is that asking too much?

LENORA. He won't even buy you flowers?

YOLANDE. I ain't seen none yet.

LENORA. You give a man a lil trim, least he can do is buy you some flowers. You did give him some trim, didn't you?

YOLANDE. Why you always asking me that?

LENORA. Damn, Yolande, I thought you was ready to do this.

YOLANDE. I am ready.

LENORA. Don't sound like it to me.

YOLANDE. I can't think about nothing else. No matter what I'm doing, walking down the street, I imagine what it's gonna be like to touch him. To touch his chest, his arms, his hands. My God. Have you seen his hands? They're huge.

LENORA. Seen them? I've had dreams about them.

YOLANDE. I wanna touch those hands. I wanna kiss those hands.

LENORA. Then what's the problem?

YOLANDE. I wanna touch and kiss and all he wants to do is hump and bump.

LENORA. Sounds to me like he wants to do the exact same thing you wanna do.

YOLANDE. I want romance, Lenora. I want flowers.

LENORA. Did you ask him for some flowers?

YOLANDE. Shouldn't have to ask him.

LENORA. Damn, Yolande. You gotta ask the man for what you want. Man won't know what you want unless you tell him.

YOLANDE. What am I supposed to do? Write out directions?

LENORA. That's one way to do it.

YOLANDE. A set of rules about what he's supposed to do?

LENORA. Step by step, in explicit detail.

YOLANDE. That would ruin it.

LENORA. Ruin what?

YOLANDE. If a man do something for me, I want him to do it 'cause he wants to do it. Not because he's following some instructions.

LENORA. Ain't nothing wrong with a lil instruction. Especially detailed instruction. You want the man to bring you flowers, you got to tell him what kind of flowers you like and how often you expect to get them. You want him to whisper some sweet words to you in the middle of the night, first thing you got to do is teach him how to talk, then turn out the lights and ease his lips over to your ear while you softly whisper to him. You got to tell him where to touch and when. Got to tell him how hard, how soft, how fast, how slow. Got to let him know when to stop moving all together and how to hold it right there. You want a man to do these things for you, you got to tell him, Yolande.

(COUNTEE enters with a bouquet of flowers.)

COUNTEE. Excuse me. Your mother said you were here and I should come right in. I didn't know you had company.

YOLANDE. It's all right. We were just talking.

COUNTEE. I can wait...

YOLANDE. No, I'm ready.

COUNTEE. I brought these for you. *(He presents the flowers.)*

YOLANDE. How sweet. Thank you.

COUNTEE. You're welcome. Ready?

YOLANDE. Oh yes. I'm ready.

Scene Four

Later that night. COUNTEE and YOLANDE enter into the foyer outside the door to the apartment. A barefoot YOLANDE carries her shoes.

COUNTEE. You okay?

YOLANDE. I think I danced up a blister on my foot.

COUNTEE. I think I have a blister on both of my feet.

YOLANDE. And you're still perspiring.

COUNTEE. Perspiring? Yolande, I am sweating like a race horse.

YOLANDE. That's what you get for commandeering the dance floor at the Sugar Cane.

COUNTEE. I was just trying to keep up with you.

YOLANDE. I haven't danced that hard in a very long time.

COUNTEE. I haven't danced that hard since I was in Paris.

YOLANDE. Paris?

COUNTEE. Oh yeah. There's this dance hall in Paris.

YOLANDE. I know. Dance halls all over Paris.

COUNTEE. But there's this one in particular. On the Left Bank. Near the old Latin Quarter...

YOLANDE. Bal Blomet?

COUNTEE. You know Bal Blomet?

YOLANDE. The doorman's name is Michel.

COUNTEE. Yes.

YOLANDE. Negro from Martinique.

COUNTEE. You know Michel.

YOLANDE. And he knows me. Last time I was there, he remembered who I was. Remembered my name.

COUNTEE. This is divine prophesy.

YOLANDE. It's my favorite place to dance when I go dancing in Paris.

COUNTEE. It's a wonder we haven't run into each other.

YOLANDE. Wouldn't that be something? Run into each other while hopping at the stomp shop at Bal Blomet.

COUNTEE. Yeah, that would be something.

YOLANDE. You been there a lot?

COUNTEE. To Bal Blomet?

YOLANDE. To Paris.

COUNTEE. Twice. Went once with my father and once with a friend of mine.

YOLANDE. Harold Jackman?

COUNTEE. You know Harold?

YOLANDE. Oh yeah. Tall, black, good-looking man?

COUNTEE. You know Harold.

YOLANDE. Extremely good-looking.

COUNTEE. Be careful because he's also quite the lady's man.

YOLANDE. And you went to Paris with your father?

COUNTEE. My father loves to travel.

YOLANDE. And you travel with him?

COUNTEE. The first trip my father and I took together was home from the hospital right after I was born and we've been traveling together ever since.

YOLANDE. I want to go there on my honeymoon.

COUNTEE. To Paris?

YOLANDE. I want to sail first class. During the day I wanna sit on the deck with my husband and sip champagne. And at night...

COUNTEE. Oh yeah.

YOLANDE. You know that you can never, under any circumstances, tell my father that you and I went dancing on the first date.

COUNTEE. Believe me. I know.

YOLANDE. He finds out that we went dancing and he'll have you locked up and me put away.

COUNTEE. You don't have to worry. It'll be our little secret.

YOLANDE. You want to come in for a drink?

COUNTEE. I would like to, but your mother...

YOLANDE. My mother's gonna have to get used to the idea that I have men calling on me.

COUNTEE. You consider me to be a caller?

YOLANDE. I'm sorry. I didn't mean to assume...

COUNTEE. No, it's all right. We've known each other for so long, I didn't know how you considered me.

YOLANDE. How do you want me to consider you?

COUNTEE. If I was one of your callers, I'd probably be last in a long line of men.

YOLANDE. That's not true.

COUNTEE. That I would be the last or that the line is long?

YOLANDE. Neither.

COUNTEE. That's not what I heard.

YOLANDE. What've you heard?

COUNTEE. I heard you were notorious.

YOLANDE. Notorious?

COUNTEE. A regular heartbreaking Aphrodite. Leaving a long littered trail of brokenhearted men.

YOLANDE. I don't know where you heard that but you heard wrong.

COUNTEE. Then why does your mother get so upset?

YOLANDE. My mother has a nervous disposition, Countee. She worries about things that are not real. She sees things that are not there. I think she needs a brain doctor but Daddy won't get her a brain doctor. He seems to think that her behavior is normal.

COUNTEE. Sorry.

YOLANDE. You wanna come in or not?

COUNTEE. I really should get going.

YOLANDE. And you call me a heartbreaker. You're the one, Mister son of a preacher man.

COUNTEE. What?

YOLANDE. I know about you. I peeped your cards.

COUNTEE. And what did you see when you peeped my cards?

OLANDE. Copper Sun. Timid Lover.

> I who employ a poet's tongue,
> Would tell you how
> You are a golden damson hung
> Upon a silver bough.

COUNTEE. You've read my work.

YOLANDE. Every woman in Harlem has read your work. They lay awake at night dreaming of being your wife. And you're such a cucumber, you act as if they don't even exist. What is it with you?

COUNTEE. Maybe I've been saving myself.

YOLANDE. For who?

COUNTEE. Somebody special.

YOLANDE. She better get here quick.

COUNTEE. Maybe she's already here. Maybe she just arrived.

YOLANDE. You trying to sweet-talk me, Countee Cullen?

COUNTEE. I'm afraid I'm not doing a very good job of it.

YOLANDE. You're doing just fine. But you know my father wants to meet the parents of any man that I'm seeing.

COUNTEE. I know.

YOLANDE. And somebody told me you were adopted.

COUNTEE. Where'd you hear that?

YOLANDE. I just heard it.

COUNTEE. Negroes won't let you rest for one minute, I swear. Just 'cause you operate in the public eye, Negroes think that your entire life should be laid open and placed on a buffet table for them to pick over.

YOLANDE. I'm sorry.

COUNTEE. I get so tired of the rumors.

YOLANDE. I apologize, Countee. I shouldn't have said anything. It was stupid.

COUNTEE. It's not your fault. You heard a rumor. Am I right?

YOLANDE. I heard a rumor.

COUNTEE. And what other rumors did you hear?

YOLANDE. Just that you were adopted.

COUNTEE. Just wait. You'll hear others.

YOLANDE. I shouldn't have repeated it.

COUNTEE. I'm gonna tell you this because I feel as if I can trust you, Yolande. I mean, I can trust you, can't I?

YOLANDE. Of course you can trust me.

COUNTEE. It's true. I was adopted. The Cullens are not my real parents.

YOLANDE. Then the story about your father bringing you home from the hospital?

COUNTEE. Is true. I was adopted as an infant. My mother died in childbirth. I never talk about it because I don't think I should have to talk about it. People think that because I'm a poet, I'm like Langston. That I should plunder the details of my life for fodder for my poetry. But I'm not like Langston. I don't care to share every embarrassing little detail of my life with the entire world. Everyone has something in their life that they would like to keep private, whether it be a very personal thought or desire, or perhaps it's a memory or single moment from the past. Well this is my private memory, the single moment from my past that I have never cared to share with anyone other than the very few people who are close to me. I hope I can now include you in that circle.

YOLANDE. Of course you can.

COUNTEE. I had hoped I could.

YOLANDE. I guess this means that now, we both have secrets.

COUNTEE. I should go.

YOLANDE. I've had a wonderful evening.

COUNTEE. So did I.

YOLANDE. And I do consider you to be a serious caller. Is that all right?

COUNTEE. That suits me just fine, Miss Du Bois.

YOLANDE. I suppose you want to kiss me good night now.

COUNTEE. I would very much like to kiss you good night. However, there are pleasures in this world that are far greater than those of carnal pleasure. Like the memory of your smile. The cocoa smooth curve of your cheekbone, or the way the corner of your mouth curls when you laugh. These are the ethereal pleasures I would like to take with me and keep until we see each other again.

(COUNTEE puts his index finger to his lips, then to hers. He exits. She swoons, regains her composure and moves into the apartment to find NINA waiting.)

YOLANDE. I should have known.

NINA. You were with that boy, weren't you?

YOLANDE. Actually...

NINA. The poet.

YOLANDE. It's none of your business who I was with.

NINA. That boy is just like your father.

YOLANDE. And what's wrong with that?

NINA. Your father groomed him.

YOLANDE. You make it sound dirty.

NINA. You don't understand your father.

YOLANDE. I understand him far better than you ever will.

NINA. You think.

YOLANDE. I see nothing wrong with going out with a man like my father, because I happen to love my father.

NINA. You are placing your head right into the jaws of the beast.

YOLANDE. Mother, please...

NINA. You don't understand the nature of the beast, Yolande. The beast is blind and the beast is greedy...

YOLANDE. I had a wonderful evening...

NINA. This beast is insatiable.

YOLANDE. I am not in the mood to hear this tonight.

NINA. And you're placing your head right into its hungry gaping mouth.

YOLANDE. There is no beast, Mother. It doesn't exist. There's nothing under the bed. There's nothing hiding in the closet. There is nothing there, Mother. Nothing's gonna gobble me up. Nothing's gonna eat me.

NINA. Just like Burghardt.

YOLANDE. Nothing like Burghardt. I'm not like Burghardt, Mother. I am not gonna die.

NINA. Is that what you think? That Burghardt died?

YOLANDE. Jesus...

NINA. That's what your father told you, isn't it?

YOLANDE. Nobody told me, Mother, this is what everybody knows. Burghardt died when he was seventeen months old.

NINA. Your brother didn't die, Yolande.

YOLANDE. He died of diphtheria, Mother.

NINA. That's what they want you to believe. But I know better. I was there. Remember?

YOLANDE. God...

NINA. Burghardt did not die of diphtheria.

YOLANDE. Please help me.

NINA. Burghardt was sacrificed. By your father. Your father sacrificed his only son.

YOLANDE. Daddy loved Burghardt, Mother.

NINA. Of course he loved him. I never said your father didn't love him. Your father loved that boy fiercely. Just like Abraham loved his son, Isaac. But when God asked Abraham to sacrifice Isaac, Abraham didn't think twice, did he? He didn't think twice.

YOLANDE. Mother, please...

NINA. Abraham built himself an altar, then placed his son upon that altar and with his hand picked up a knife to slay his son that he loved so fiercely. Both Burghardt and Isaac were placed upon the altar. Only difference, Burghardt received no last-minute reprieve. There was no intervening angel to appear on Burghardt's behalf. No. The voice of God was conspicuously silent when Burghardt was sacrificed. There were no angels singing. No booming voice of God coming down from on high to save my Burghardt with the golden-spun hair. There was nothing but me and Burghardt laying there waiting for your father to come home. Me and Burghardt with the golden-spun hair whose body had grown cold.

YOLANDE. Would you like your medicine, Mother?

NINA. Your father sacrificed my only son.

YOLANDE. Would you like a headache powder?

NINA. And now he's about to sacrifice you.

Scene Five

JIMMY and LENORA in the rehearsal hall.

JIMMY. Where is she?

LENORA. I don't know.

JIMMY. Six-thirty.

LENORA. I know what time it is.

JIMMY. She ain't here.

LENORA. I can see that.

JIMMY. What she say?

LENORA. She said she was gonna meet us.

JIMMY. What time?

LENORA. I already told you.

JIMMY. Tell me again.

LENORA. She said she was gonna meet us at six o'clock.

JIMMY. And now it's six-thirty.

LENORA. I know, Jimmy.

JIMMY. So where the hell is she?

LENORA. Damn, Jimmy. What did I just tell you? I don't know where she is.

JIMMY. Then maybe you can tell me this: What's the nigger's name?

LENORA. What nigger?

JIMMY. The nigger she been messing with.

LENORA. She ain't messing with nobody.

JIMMY. Don't try to give me that tissue-paper lie.

LENORA. Not that I…I know of.

JIMMY. You can't lie, Lenora, not to me. I can read you like a piece of sheet music. .

LENORA. I...I'm not lying.

JIMMY. See? There you go. You get that yammer in your voice. Every time you tell a lie.

LENORA. I...I...

JIMMY. You gettin' ready to tell a big one.

LENORA. Shit!

JIMMY. What's the nigger's name?

LENORA. Honest to God, Jimmy. I...I do not know if she's seeing somebody else or not.

JIMMY. I tell you what, I find out who he is, I'm gonna scramble his ass like a pair 'a fresh country eggs.

LENORA. You ain't got to do all of that.

JIMMY. You know who it is, don't you?

LENORA. All you got to do is talk to her every now and then. Treat her nice.

JIMMY. I talk to her. Hell, I treat her nice.

LENORA. When was the last time you bought her some flowers?

JIMMY. Flowers?

LENORA. They look like collard greens with little decorations on top.

JIMMY. Don't get smart with me.

LENORA. When was the last time you bought her some flowers, Jimmy?

JIMMY. She ain't said nothing to me about buying her some flowers.

LENORA. Some things, a woman shouldn't have to ask for.

JIMMY. She ain't got no problem asking for everything else she want. She wanted me to find a new stack. I found a new stack. Got a nice kitchenette, real nice, two rooms on 110th Street. You think she been around to see it? Hell naw. I ain't seen her. She's out running around with some other nigger. She wants to get on a boat and sail first class to Paris. Well, I can't afford no goddamn first-class honeymoon in Paris.

LENORA. When'd you get a new place to live?

JIMMY. Few days ago.

LENORA. I thought you were broke.

JIMMY. I was broke.

LENORA. Then where'd you get the money?

JIMMY. Who you supposed to be? Policeman, wanna know where I got my money?

(YOLANDE enters.)

JIMMY. Well if it ain't the queen of Sheba, coming here to grace us with her presence.

YOLANDE. Excuse me?

JIMMY. What did we do, Almighty Queen, to deserve to be in your company?

YOLANDE. I came here thinking we were gonna go have some dinner after you were done with rehearsal but apparently I was mistaken.

LENORA. How you doing, Yolande?

YOLANDE. I'm fine. How about you?

JIMMY. Thought you was going back to Baltimore for a job interview.

YOLANDE. I went back to Baltimore for a job interview. Went back last week.

JIMMY. Told me you was going three weeks ago.

YOLANDE. And right after I told you that, I found out that my father was coming home and I decided to stay here and see him.

JIMMY. Why didn't you tell me?

YOLANDE. I'm telling you now, Jimmy.

JIMMY. Why couldn't you tell me before?

YOLANDE. Before what?

JIMMY. Before you decided to go out to the Sugar Cane and stay till two a.m. tearing up the dance floor with some nigger. That's before what. Now after you pick your mouth up off the floor, I want you to tell me one thang: What's the nigger's name?

YOLANDE. That ain't nothing for you to worry about.

JIMMY. Tell me the nigger's name and let me decide whether or not to worry.

YOLANDE. He's a friend.

JIMMY. Apparently.

YOLANDE. A friend of my father's.

JIMMY. I don't care whose friend he is. I wanna know the nigger's name.

YOLANDE. Nothing happened between us, Jimmy. He's like a cousin to me.

JIMMY. Is he a man?

YOLANDE. Is he a what?

JIMMY. A man. Either he's a man or he's not. If he's a man, friend of the family, cousin, uncle, third nephew removed, I don't care what, you got no business being out dancing with him till two o'clock in the morning.

YOLANDE. Every time a man and a woman get together, they don't have to be thinking about all that mess that you always thinking about.

JIMMY. Did he tell you that? That bullshit? Let me tell you sumthin'. Everytime a man and a woman get together, they only thinking about one thing. Getting nasty. Am I right? Lenora? Am I right?

LENORA. Well, I...I...uh...

JIMMY. 'Course I'm right. You take a man, you take a woman, put them together and unless they brother and sister, they thinking about getting nasty with each other. And in some parts of this world, I hear it don't even matter if they brother and sister. They get nasty with each other anyway.

YOLANDE. We're not in some parts of the world. We're in Harlem, and in Harlem, not all men are thinking about that.

JIMMY. That what the nigger tell you? That he wasn't like that? That he was different?

YOLANDE. Not every man in this world is like you, Jimmy.

JIMMY. If he tried to tell you he was different, he was lying to you, Yolande. I been on this earth for a very long time and I'm here to tell you that man's hunger is eternal. A man will always be attracted to the sway of a woman's hip and to the curve of a woman's breast. It ain't a choice that the man makes, the man can't help it, it's the way the man is made. I don't care who he is, where he come from or where he think he's going, every time a man looks at a woman, he's thinking about only one thang and that's getting himself some juice. The only time he ain't thinking about getting himself some juice is right after he done got himself some juice. And there ain't nothing you or anybody else can do to change that. Everything that a man does in his life, whether he's playing some music, building a house, sporting some clean vines, working a job, or taking a bath, he doing it for only one reason: To get himself some juice. Getting juice is a man's number one priority in life.

YOLANDE. You are so vulgar.

JIMMY. His number two priority in life is making sure some other nigger don't come along and take his juice away.

YOLANDE. So now you trying to tell me that even jealously is natural?

JIMMY. As natural as a warm summer rain. I'm talking about survival of the fittest. See? Your old man ain't the only educated nigger around here.

YOLANDE. Jealously is not natural, Jimmy.

JIMMY. It's part of human nature, Yolande. You don't like it, your argument ain't with me. It's with the man upstairs.

YOLANDE. I got a telegram for you. Human civilization has advanced beyond the Stone Age. We are no longer hunters and gatherers. There are pleasures in this world that are far greater than those of carnal pleasure.

JIMMY. What kind of shit is that?

YOLANDE. What?

JIMMY. Pleasures greater than carnal—what's this nigger's name?

YOLANDE. I'm not telling you.

JIMMY. Ain't I done right by you? Ain't I tried to give you everything that you ask for? You ask me to find a new place to live. I found a new place to live. You didn't even know that, did you? No, you didn't even know. I got a two-room kitchenette, separated by a door that you can close if you want.

YOLANDE. I didn't ask you to do that for me.

JIMMY. You told me you didn't like the place I was staying.

YOLANDE. I didn't tell you to go out and find another place.

JIMMY. What you expect me to do? Stay in a place that you don't like? And look at this. Look what else I got for you. *(He produces a small ring box.)* Here.

YOLANDE. What is this supposed to be?

JIMMY. Supposed to be a ring.

LENORA. Let me see.

JIMMY. I was gonna give it to you tonight but you might as well have it now.

YOLANDE. Where'd you get the money for this?

JIMMY. Don't you worry about it. Point is, I done right by you. I give you everything you ask for. Still can't afford no goddamn honeymoon in Paris, but I'm working on it.

YOLANDE. Where'd you get the money for the ring, Jimmy?

LENORA. I'll tell you where. The band ain't been paid for the past three weeks. That's where he got the money.

YOLANDE. You spend that money you were supposed to use to pay the band?

JIMMY. Everybody's gonna get paid.

YOLANDE. When?

JIMMY. Everybody's gonna get every dime that's coming to them.

YOLANDE. When, Jimmy?

LENORA. You have to admit, this is a gorgeous ring.

JIMMY. Soon as we get that gig at the Cotton Club.

LENORA. A diamond and two sapphires.

JIMMY. We get that gig at the Cotton Club, everybody gonna be rolling in dough.

YOLANDE. You talk to the man at the Cotton Club?

LENORA. Look at that. My size and everything.

JIMMY. Not yet.

YOLANDE. Then how you know you gonna get the job?

JIMMY. I can feel it.

YOLANDE. You can feel it?

JIMMY. In my bones.

LENORA. You better hope that's not just a touch of bursitis.

JIMMY. Ain't no goddamn bursitis. I've figured it all out. I've discovered the thing that distinguishes us from the other bands. Lenora knows. Tell her, Lenora.

YOLANDE. I can't accept that ring, Jimmy.

JIMMY. What you mean you can't accept it?

YOLANDE. You spending money that ain't yours to spend. Take this back to where you got it and get your money back. Then take that money and do what you was supposed to do with it and pay the men in your band, Jimmy.

JIMMY. Yolande…

YOLANDE. No. Pay the men in your band.

Scene Six

The Du Bois apartment. WILL and COUNTEE enter.

WILL. Fine meal. Yes sir, very fine meal. Wife is a very good cook. Don't you think?

COUNTEE. Yes sir.

WILL. She received excellent household training from her mother and in turn, has done everything in her power to pass on those skills to Yolande. And while I cannot personally vouch for Yolande's culinary dexterity I would be negligent if I failed to point out that she is her mother's daughter and if you enjoyed the meal you just had, remember that the apple never falls far from the tree. Would you like a glass of wine?

COUNTEE. Wine?

WILL. A Rhine I purchased while I was in Berlin. Ordinarily I do not partake of alcoholic beverages which dull the senses, especially American whiskeys which I find to have the taste and texture of formaldehyde. However, this wine is singular in its purpose and character. It's German, made from a special hybrid grape which the Germans developed after years of careful crossbreeding. You see, that's the secret of superior quality. Careful crossbreeding. Care to join me?

COUNTEE. I'd be honored.

WILL. You and Yolande seem to have hit it off quite well.

COUNTEE. Yes sir.

WILL. Dinner, the theater. I even understand that you two went out dancing together on your first date.

COUNTEE. How did you...

WILL. Very little escapes me, Countee. I know everything worth knowing.

COUNTEE. With your permission, sir, I would like to ask Yolande to marry me.

WILL. Why? Because you love her? Or because you think it's the right thing to do?

COUNTEE. I think that Yolande has all the attributes that I'm looking for in a wife. I also believe that she and I have many things in common and that we're very well matched, Dr. Du Bois.

WILL. In that case, you don't need to ask me for my permission. You want the girl to marry you? Ask the girl to marry you.

COUNTEE. But what do you think? If I asked her?

WILL. I think if we announced to the world that Countee Cullen was to marry the daughter of W.E.B. Du Bois, it would create such a sensation that your marriage would be the marriage of the decade. It would represent the prefect union of Negro talent, brains and beauty. It would shatter old stereotypes of the Negro in this country. The walls of prejudice would come crashing down. It would be a star in the pinnacle of the Harlem Renaissance. However, you mustn't allow any of this to influence your decision, Countee. First and foremost in my mind is your work and my daughter's happiness. However, you also might be interested in knowing that I've spoken with the foundation regarding your fellowship. They asked me for a written recommendation which I've already completed. *(He offers COUNTEE an envelope.)* As soon as the foundation receives this recommendation, you'll receive your fellowship. I believe this fulfils my part of the agreement.

(YOLANDE enters with plates.)

YOLANDE. Everybody ready for dessert?

WILL. What're we having?

YOLANDE. Peach cobbler and pecan pie.

WILL. I'll have the cobbler. Countee?

COUNTEE. No peaches for me. I'll have the pecan.

YOLANDE. Pecan pie it is.

WILL. I'll get it. You have a guest. Entertain him. *(Exits.)*

YOLANDE. How'd you like the dinner?

COUNTEE. It was very good.

YOLANDE. My mother may be a bit daft but she knows how to cook. Me? I can't even boil water.

COUNTEE. Guess what? I have some good news.

YOLANDE. So do I.

COUNTEE. You first.

YOLANDE. Okay. I got the job in Baltimore. I'm gonna be teaching high school. This is the beginning of my career.

COUNTEE. Congratulations.

YOLANDE. Thank you. Now you, what's your news?

COUNTEE. I'm going back to Paris, but this time, I'll probably be gone for at least a year.

YOLANDE. Lucky you.

COUNTEE. And I want you to go with me, Yolande.

YOLANDE. To Paris?

COUNTEE. During the day we can sit on the deck sipping champagne and at night…

YOLANDE. Yeah, right. You and me. Sailing to Paris. Together. Unchaperoned. Wouldn't that be a scandal?

COUNTEE. Wouldn't be if we were married.

YOLANDE. To each other?

COUNTEE. I like being with you, Yolande. We know each other and I feel as if I can trust you. We trust each other and we have fun when we're together. You wanna go back to Paris. We can go back together.

YOLANDE. Are you proposing marriage to me?

COUNTEE. If you can promise me one thing. If you can promise me that, if we got married, things between us would not change. If you can stand in the center of your heart and swear to me that you would do everything in your power to freeze this moment in time, to preserve as we are now, for the rest of our lives...

YOLANDE. I wouldn't want anything between us to change.

COUNTEE. Then yes, I am proposing to you. Yolande, will you marry me?

YOLANDE. Countee...

COUNTEE. You don't have to answer now. Think about it. Think about all the things you want to do. Think about Paris.

YOLANDE. I've been seeing someone else.

COUNTEE. My faith in human goodness would be shattered if there were not at least one other man competing for your affections.

YOLANDE. This other man I've been seeing, we've been together for a very long time.

COUNTEE. You had a life before you met me, just as I had a life before I met you. I'm not asking you to change that.

YOLANDE. He and I are very close, Countee.

COUNTEE. Is he your lover?

YOLANDE. No. Lover? Heavens no. He's a friend, Countee. He's a very good friend.

COUNTEE. If he's a friend, then you must promise me that you will keep him as a friend. Even if you and I are married.

YOLANDE. That would be impossible.

COUNTEE. Good friends are like precious jewels. They're very rare and very hard to find. Once you find one that's authentic, you should keep it, hold onto it, and cherish it because you never know when or if, indeed, you'll ever find another. For example, Harold Jackman's a good friend of mine and I would never sever my relationship with him. Likewise, I would not expect you to sever your relationship with your friend even if we were married.

YOLANDE. You wouldn't be jealous?

COUNTEE. Why would I be jealous?

YOLANDE. All men are jealous. It's human nature.

COUNTEE. Most men I know are very sophisticated. They understand that a fully rounded and complete life consists of many different elements and many different people. That spectrum includes trust but it also includes very good friends.

YOLANDE. What about my job in Baltimore?

COUNTEE. If you want to teach high school in Baltimore, Yolande, I suggest that you teach high school in Baltimore. Our marriage should not interfere with the development of your vocation. Remember, our goal here is to keep things as they are.

(WILL enters.)

WILL. Pecan pie for Countee. And what're you having, Yolande?

YOLANDE. I would like some peaches.

WILL. The pecan pie is better. How about some pecans?

COUNTEE. I'll get it.

WILL. No, I'll get it.

COUNTEE. Please. Allow me. *(Exits.)*

WILL. What'd you do? Ouchie? What happened?

YOLANDE. Nothing happened, Daddy.

WILL. What did you say to him?

YOLANDE. I didn't say anything. He asked me to marry him.

WILL. Congratulations. My girl's getting married. *(He calls out:)* Wife! Get in here! Congratulations, Ouchie. Wife!

YOLANDE. He asked me to marry him, Daddy. I didn't say I would.

WILL. But you will, right? Ouchie? Did you tell him no?

YOLANDE. I wanted to talk to you first.

WILL. Good choice. Very good. Now listen to me, Ouchie. It is impossible for me to love you any more than I already do. And it is through my love for you that I tell you that you and Countee are two of a kind. You're of the same breeding, the same stock. Marrying Countee Cullen is one of the best things you could ever do.

YOLANDE. Then why do I feel so uncertain?

WILL. You're moving into unchartered area, Ouchie, into a land which you've never before explored. It's natural for you to feel a bit apprehensive. The question is: Do you love him?

YOLANDE. Shouldn't I feel something?

WILL. You should.

YOLANDE. But I don't.

WILL. That's not surprising. You're probably a bit confused.

YOLANDE. I care for him, Daddy.

WILL. That's good.

YOLANDE. But I do not love him.

WILL. Love is not a lightning bolt that strikes in the middle of a storm. It's not a panacea that will wash away all of your pain and worries. If anything, love is like a very slow-burning fire that may smolder for years before finally catching ablaze. I want you to be happy, Yolande. Please don't wait for lightning to strike.

(NINA enters with desserts followed by LENORA and COUNTEE.)

NINA. Yolande, I thought you wanted peach cobbler?
YOLANDE. That is what I wanted.
NINA. Then why is Countee bringing you pecan pie?

(JIMMY has entered into the foyer and now rings the bell. NINA moves to the door and looks through the peephole.)

LENORA. You ought to get yourself a piece of that cobbler. I'm here to testify, those peaches are good. This here is my third piece. But then again, the pecan ain't so bad either.
NINA. It's that man.
WILL. What man?
NINA. Yolande's friend. The musician.
LENORA. Oh-oh.
NINA. Looking for Yolande.
WILL. We're in the middle of a family dinner.
NINA. What should I do?
WILL. Are you expecting him, Yolande?
YOLANDE. No.
WILL. Then why is he here?
YOLANDE. I don't know, Daddy.
NINA. What do you want me to do, Will?
WILL. I'll take care of it.
YOLANDE. No, I'll do it.

WILL. You sure?

NINA. Yolande, let your father take care of it.

WILL. Wife, Yolande can handle herself. She's a grown, mature woman. It's time for her to start making decisions on her own.

LENORA *(to COUNTEE)*. Can you box?

COUNTEE. Can I what?

LENORA. Throw down. Stick and jab, bob and weave, 'cause if not, if I was you, I'd find me someplace to hide.

(YOLANDE opens the door.)

JIMMY. Hey, baby. Hope I'm not disturbing...

YOLANDE. What do you want, Jimmy?

JIMMY. I know this is not...

YOLANDE. What d'you want?

JIMMY. Ain't you gonna invite me in?

YOLANDE. Now's not a good time.

JIMMY. I just wanted to stop by to give you...

YOLANDE. You're interrupting a family dinner.

JIMMY. I'm sorry. I hadn't seen you, I wanted to give you this. *(He hands her a small box.)*

YOLANDE. What is it?

JIMMY. You know what it is. Open it. I talked to the man from the Lafayette. He's gonna book us for the next six weeks. You know what that means? That means we ain't got to go to Cleveland or Dayton. We can stay here in New York. Well? Open it.

WILL. Yolande?

JIMMY. I bought it with my own money. That was after I paid every dime I owed to every swinging dick in the band.

YOLANDE. Jimmy…

JIMMY. I know, I know. Lenora already told me. I gotta talk to your daddy first. And I plan to do right by you, Yolande, so that's the reason I'm here, to talk to your daddy. I still ain't walking around carrying no damned silver-tipped walking stick, but I'll talk to the man. Where is he? *(JIMMY pushes inside.)* Sorry. Looks like I'm interrupting a party or something.

WILL. You're interrupting a very personal family gathering, young man.

JIMMY. Sorry. *(To YOLANDE.)* All right, baby, I'll see you tomorrow and we'll— *(He sees COUNTEE.)* Who's that? That's him, ain't it? That's the other nigger you been seeing.

WILL. See here, young man…

YOLANDE. Jimmy, you're outta line.

JIMMY. I'm outta line? You sitting up here with some other nigger and you calling me outta line?

YOLANDE. We'll talk about this tomorrow.

JIMMY. What you mean tomorrow? Ain't no tomorrow. We gonna straighten this shit out today. Right here and now.

YOLANDE. Jimmy, please.

JIMMY. That's him, ain't it?

YOLANDE. If you'd wait till later, I can explain everything.

JIMMY. Ain't no later.

LENORA *(to YOLANDE)*. Don't try to hide behind me.

JIMMY. I want an explanation now.

LENORA. He's not gonna kill me trying to get to you.

JIMMY. Who the hell is he, Yolande?

WILL. See here, young man. My daughter is not beholding to you or any other man.

JIMMY. I'm gonna ask you one more time, Yolande.

YOLANDE. Why you got to do this, Jimmy? Why you got to come in here and ruin everything?

JIMMY. Why you got to keep playing me for a fool?

YOLANDE. Ain't nobody playing you for a fool. If you just wait till later...

JIMMY. I'm not waiting for later. I'm sick of this. I'm sick of sniffing up behind you like a little dog while you flash your precious little tail all over town. I'm sick of begging you, I'm sick of waiting for you while you try to figure out what you gonna do. Ain't no later, Yolande. You're gonna have to make up your mind right here and now. You're gonna have to choose between me and that nigger over there.

YOLANDE. In that case, I already made up my mind.

JIMMY. Good.

YOLANDE. I appreciate your gift but I can't accept it. I'm getting married, Jimmy. I'm getting married to Countee Cullen.

JIMMY. To who?

YOLANDE. Now if you don't mind, we're in the middle of a family dinner.

JIMMY. You gonna marry this nigger?

YOLANDE. And I'd appreciate it if you would leave.

JIMMY. This ain't right.

WILL. You've been asked to leave, young man.

JIMMY. Come on, Yolande. Go with me. Let's take a walk.

YOLANDE. No.

JIMMY. We can talk about this...

YOLANDE. There's nothing to talk about.

WILL. You've been asked to leave.

JIMMY. Tomorrow. We'll talk tomorrow.

YOLANDE. No, Jimmy.

JIMMY. Come with me. Come and look at the apartment...

YOLANDE. Listen to me.

JIMMY. We'll stop and get some coffee...

YOLANDE. It's over, Jimmy. I'm getting married.

JIMMY. Lenora, do something.

YOLANDE. I want you outta my house.

JIMMY. Talk to her.

YOLANDE. You understand what I'm saying to you?

JIMMY. Help me. Lenora, please.

YOLANDE. Get out.

JIMMY. Lenora...

YOLANDE. Go away, Jimmy. I don't wanna ever see you again. Understand? I hate you. Get out.

JIMMY. All right, Yolande.

YOLANDE. Get out.

JIMMY. All right. Okay. I'm leaving. I'm gone. *(Exits.)*

WILL. Good girl.

NINA. Yolande's getting married?

WILL. You did good.

NINA. My little girl's getting married.

End of Act One

ACT TWO

Scene One

Du Bois apartment. NINA and YOLANDE. NINA arranges flowers in a vase.

NINA. Miss Otis was by the other day. Ten weeks later and she is still talking about your wedding. But I'm not surprised. Everybody in Harlem is still talking about your wedding. Ten ushers in black tie and tails. Sixteen bridesmaids in dresses that were gorgeous, Yolande, just gorgeous up to heaven. Miss Otis still can't get over how many flowers were at the church. Roses and orchids and tulips and lilies. She said she had never seen so many flowers in one place before. She said it looked like the Garden of Eden. How she would know what the Garden of Eden looks like, I don't know, I'm just telling you what she said. You know what Mrs. Pingree said? Mrs. Pingree said that she thought there were too many flowers. Said it looked like somebody's funeral instead of a wedding, looked like somebody had died. But she's just jealous 'cause she didn't receive an invitation. I tried to explain to her that there wasn't enough room to invite everybody to the wedding. As it was, there were over one thousand people at the church that day. We sent out invitations to only five hundred because the church only seats five hundred. Your father was not happy with the prospect of providing food and drink for

five hundred people, but when I saw your father standing at that altar with you on his left and Countee on the
right, and I saw the pride bursting from your father's
face as he looked out over the church full of Negro art-
ists, politicians, businessmen and dignitaries from all
across the country, I realized that your father would
have gladly spent twice as much for that moment. That
moment, for him, will always be frozen in time. *(She
finishes the arrangement.)* There. That's very nice, don't
you think? Yolande? You okay? Would you like me to
make you some tea?

YOLANDE. When did you say Daddy was gonna be
home?

NINA. Not for another week. He's in Philadelphia, I think.
Yes, Philadelphia. Either that or Washington, I'm not
quite sure. I get a little confused every now and then.
And where did you say Countee was?

YOLANDE. He's in Boston, Mother.

NINA. Boston? Did I already ask you that?

YOLANDE. Yes, you did.

NINA. I'm sorry. Would you like me to make you a cup of tea?

YOLANDE. No, Mother. Thank you.

NINA. Miss Otis said that green tea will help ease your
morning sickness.

YOLANDE. I don't have morning sickness.

NINA. Who do you think you're kidding, Yolande. I heard
you having difficulties this morning.

YOLANDE. Difficulties?

NINA. In the bathroom. Of course, not that I was listening.

YOLANDE. It was the flowers, Mother.

NINA. The flowers?

YOLANDE. The smell of the flowers made me sick.

NINA. Sounds like morning sickness to me.

YOLANDE. I'm sick of smelling them, I'm sick of looking at them, I'm sick of thinking about them…

NINA. Let me make you a cup of tea.

YOLANDE. Didn't I tell you I didn't want any of your damned tea?

NINA. I hope this attitude of yours is not indicative of the next nine months, 'cause if so, we're gonna be in for a very long and bumpy ride.

YOLANDE. What is it with you? Why do you always see things that are not there?

NINA. I don't know, Yolande. Why do you have such a problem seeing things that are standing right in front of you?

YOLANDE. This is useless.

NINA. You know what I think?

YOLANDE. No, but I'm sure you're gonna tell me.

NINA. I think it's high time you and I had a talk.

YOLANDE. A talk?

NINA. A heart-to-heart.

YOLANDE. With you?

NINA. I am your mother.

YOLANDE. Please, don't remind me.

NINA. Have I done something to you, Yolande?

YOLANDE. I'm sorry.

NINA. Something to hurt you?

YOLANDE. I'm sorry, Mother. It's just…

NINA. You wanna talk about it?

YOLANDE. What makes you think I have something I wanna talk about?

NINA. You went on your honeymoon…

YOLANDE. Yes.

NINA. To Niagara Falls. And the falls are very romantic, Yolande.

YOLANDE. Yes, very romantic.

NINA. But you left. You came home almost a week early.

YOLANDE. Because of my job, Mother. I had to come home to prepare for my job.

NINA. I hope you're not still considering accepting that job.

YOLANDE. I've already accepted it.

NINA. You don't need a job. You already have a job. You're married, for God's sake.

YOLANDE. I don't plan to give up my professional vocation just because I got married.

NINA. What vocation? You don't have a vocation.

YOLANDE. Not yet, but I plan to have one. I plan to have a life, Mother.

NINA. You have a life.

YOLANDE. Being married is a life?

NINA. And what's wrong with that?

YOLANDE. It's not enough for me.

NINA. It was enough for me.

YOLANDE. Well, I don't plan on ending up like you.

NINA. I see. Yes, that would be the worst thing that could ever happen to you, wouldn't it?

YOLANDE. I didn't mean it like that.

NINA. I know how you meant it. I know exactly how you meant it. You don't want to end up like me for good reason. But I was not always like this. I used to be like you, you know. I used to be a soldier. I marched right into battle. Right after Burghardt was born, your father moved us to Atlanta and Atlanta was not a pretty place for Negroes to live. Everything was segregated. The parks, the theaters, public transportation, the restaurants, trains stations, even the public library was segregated. And the schools and hospitals, Negroes weren't even allowed in the schools and hospitals. Even back then I refused to patronize any system of segregation, which meant I had to walk every place I went, and since Negroes were lawfully prohibited from using any park, water fountain, or even stopping to rest on a public bench, whenever I left the house I could not stop walking, not to rest, not to get a drink of water, not for one moment, not until I had reached my destination. I pictured myself as that woman who I heard speak the other day. Gertrude Ederle. She swam from France to Great Britain, across the entire English Channel, without stopping once. That's how I felt every time I left that house in Atlanta. Like Gertrude Ederle, I had to continue to press on, I could not stop, I could not rest, not for one moment lest I drown in a sea of hate.

YOLANDE. You okay, Mother?

NINA. I find it very difficult to believe that Countee has agreed to forsake New York in favor of Baltimore.

YOLANDE. He hasn't.

NINA. Then how do you plan to teach in Baltimore?

YOLANDE. I plan to live in Baltimore, Mother.

NINA. And what is Countee supposed to do?

YOLANDE. Countee plans to stay in New York.

NINA. That doesn't make any sense.

YOLANDE. We plan to keep two apartments, Mother.

NINA. Two apartments?

YOLANDE. One in New York and one in Baltimore.

NINA. No sense at all.

YOLANDE. We don't plan to surrender to convention. We liked the way our relationship was before we were married and we plan to keep things the way they were.

NINA. Yolande, baby. Listen to me. It's not such a bad thing, being a wife. Not once you get used to it. That's the hardest part, Yolande, getting used to it. That's the part that takes a while. After your father and I were married, I cried practically ever time he touched me for almost a year. But I got used to it. Every woman has a tough time at first. But the trick is, what I've found, is to lay real still. You lay as still as you can, and try to think of something else. Maybe sing a song. Sing with the voice of your mind, sing with the voice that comes to you from somewhere deep down inside. You sing with that voice, you go ahead and let the man do his business, and it'll be over before you know it.

YOLANDE. What're you talking about?

NINA. I'm talking about tolerating your duties, Yolande. Your marital duties.

YOLANDE. You talking about sex?

NINA. There's no need for that type of language.

YOLANDE. My mother's talking to me about sex.

NINA. I'm talking about the difficulties of being a wife.

YOLANDE. Ain't this about a clock-stopper.

NINA. I know, we should have had this conversation a long time ago. If we had this conversation, maybe you and your husband wouldn't be in the midst of these difficulties.

YOLANDE. What difficulties? There are no difficulties.

NINA. You ended your honeymoon early.

YOLANDE. I've already explained that to you.

NINA. I know what you said but you have to understand how it looks.

YOLANDE. Countee and I do not have to be together every single moment of every day. You and Daddy are not together every single moment of every day and nobody talks about how that looks.

NINA. Your father is doing very important work.

YOLANDE. In case you haven't heard, my husband is doing very important work as well. Now, is there anything else you would like to know?

NINA. You're gonna have a baby, Yolande. You cannot live in Baltimore with a child while your husband lives in New York. It makes no sense. Your duty, as a wife, is to be with your husband and to, occasionally at night, tolerate your marital obligations.

YOLANDE. I'm not talking to you about this.

NINA. You're not ready yet. But you will be. And when you are ready to talk about tolerating your obligations, promise me that you'll come to me, your mother, to talk. Okay? Yolande? You promise?

Scene Two

COUNTEE and WILL in WILL's study.

WILL. I'm sorry I couldn't get back any sooner. I was detained at a NAACP meeting in Pittsburgh. Now I want you to tell me. What happened?

COUNTEE. Yolande decided to come home early.

WILL. From your honeymoon?

COUNTEE. She wanted to get back early in order to prepare for her job.

WILL. You ended your honeymoon early for a teaching job in Baltimore?

COUNTEE. She wanted to take time to prepare her lesson plans and to meet with some of the other teachers. You know Yolande. Once she makes up her mind to do something, there's nothing I can do.

WILL. And have the newspapers been notified of this fact?

COUNTEE. I don't know.

WILL. No matter what you do, no matter how you move or what you say, you must be aware of how it will appear to the public.

COUNTEE. I understand that, Dr. Du Bois.

WILL. Apparently your understanding was only marginal because you ended your honeymoon early and failed to notify the newspapers as to the reason why. Do you know what happens when you fail to supply the newspapers with facts? They make up their own facts and we cannot allow that to happen.

COUNTEE. I'm sorry. It was an oversight.

WILL. Is there anything else I should know?

COUNTEE. Like what?

WILL. Are you two having any problems?

COUNTEE. No, no problems.

WILL. I want you to feel free to confide in me.

COUNTEE. We're not having any problems, Dr. Du Bois.

WILL. What about your trip to Paris?

COUNTEE. There has been a slight change of plans but it's not a problem.

WILL. What kind of change of plans?

COUNTEE. Yolande has always wanted to travel first class and I simply cannot afford for her to travel first class.

WILL. How much do you need?

COUNTEE. I cannot, in good conscience, accept any more money from you, Dr. Du Bois.

WILL. It's not a problem, Countee. How much?

COUNTEE. No.

WILL. Countee, I consider you to be like a son to me, like my Burghardt who was taken away from me at a very young age. Many times I close my eyes and, in my mind, paint a picture of what my Burghardt would look like had he lived. I try to imagine the glow of his face, the texture of his voice, I try to imagine happiness dancing in his eyes. I must've painted a hundred different pictures of Burghardt using a hundred different faces, but every time I look at one of those faces, the face I see is not the face of Burghardt. No matter what eyes, lips and nose I use, in the end, the person I see is you. And as my son, in law and in spirit, I will gladly give you any type of assistance you will ever need, Countee, without exception, as if you were an issue of my own flesh.

COUNTEE. But it's time for Yolande and I to take responsibility for our own lives.

WILL. This marriage involves more than just you and Yolande. The future of practically every Negro in this country is enmeshed in your marriage. Do you know what this is? *(He holds up an envelope.)* This is a letter from Dr. Walter Beekman, provost at Harvard University. *(He holds up another envelope.)* Dr. Roger Crogman, president of Atlanta University. And this is from Judge Julian Mack, United States Circuit Court of New

York City. All of them expressing their heartfelt congratulations and best wishes for the bride and groom. And if you listen carefully, you will hear, somewhere off in the distance, a sound. A rumble, barely perceptible, but it's there, nevertheless. That sound you hear is the crumbling of the walls of segregation, the walls of prejudice which are about to come tumbling down. I feel a monumental change about to happen in this country and your marriage is on the *avant-garde* of that change. You cannot march into the fray alone, Countee. There's too much at stake.

COUNTEE. If I needed your help, I would gladly accept it, Dr. Du Bois. But I've already made other arrangements. My friend, Harold Jackman, has pledged to make a financial contribution to the trip to Paris. Yolande has decided not to join me in Paris until December. This way, she can spend time preparing to teach and we both can save money so that when she does join me in December, she can travel in the style to which she is accustomed. You see, Dr. Du Bois, it's all been taken care of.

WILL. And what about the newspapers?

COUNTEE. Again, an oversight.

WILL. It's an oversight we cannot afford. I'll take care of the newspapers and make sure they have all the facts.

COUNTEE. Thank you.

WILL. No need to thank me, son. I do what I do for not only you but for us all.

Scene Three

LENORA and YOLANDE.

LENORA. It was a slaughter. They never knew what hit them, never knew which way to look, never knew which way it was coming from. The first wave moved in from the left. They were marching in step, lock step, axes under their arms, moving with military precision. The second wave moved in from the right, marching in step, lock step, keeping the beat, boom pop, boom pop, boom pop pow. Suddenly dead center, Jimmy rises up from what appears to be nowhere, and make no mistake about this: Jimmy is cleaner than a broke-dick dog. White tie and tails. Ofay sitting at a table in the front fell out into the aisle. Jimmy got his ass and hadn't even played one note yet. Jimmy looks around, raises his baton, the brass raise up with him. Old wrinkled wench at a table in the back throws up her arms and falls out. Jimmy got her, still ain't played note one. Baton comes down, the band blows out the first notes of "For Dancers Only" and the place goes up for grabs. People moving thisaway and thataway. Arms, legs and sweat flying all over the dance floor. But Jimmy is not perturbed, he ain't broke a sweat. Even the razor-sharp crease in his tuxedo pants is undisturbed. He's out front of that band and he's leading, and he's listening, and he's watching them ofays on the dance floor and he's killing them with a cool calculated syncopated precision that would make a diamond cutter pack up his tools and·walk away in shame.

YOLANDE. Good for him.

LENORA. That's what I thought. But later, after the last set, after all the white folks had gone, Jimmy's looking around the room like he's searching, like he's looking for somebody. Then I realize who he's looking for. He's looking for you. But you ain't there. That's when I realized that he's still waiting for you, Yolande.

YOLANDE. Waiting for me for what?

LENORA. To make an appearance. To hear him play.

YOLANDE. I've already heard him play, more times than I care to remember.

LENORA. Then maybe he's waiting for you to tell him what happened.

YOLANDE. I got married. That's what happened. I thought he was aware of that fact.

LENORA. Why you being so hard on Jimmy?

YOLANDE. Why you got to keep bothering me about this man? Don't nobody care about him.

LENORA. You cared about him. Or at least you did at one point in time.

YOLANDE. That point in time has passed, Lenora. You are revisiting ancient history.

LENORA. Least you could do is sit down and talk to him.

YOLANDE. I am married, Lenora.

LENORA. Help ease his pain a bit. That ain't gonna kill you.

YOLANDE. Why is this so hard for you to understand? I cannot be hanging out with Jimmy Lunceford anymore.

LENORA. All right, I got it.

YOLANDE. You wanna help ease his pain? You talk to him. You help him understand.

LENORA. What's the matter with you?

YOLANDE. I thought it was gonna be different.

LENORA. You thought what was gonna be different?

YOLANDE. Everything. Being married. Being a wife. But it's not different. At least I don't feel any different.

LENORA. Is that all?

YOLANDE. I don't feel any different than I felt before.

LENORA. You are so typical.

YOLANDE. Typical?

LENORA. You think you the only woman that's going through what you going through right now? Well you're not. Women been going through what you going through since the beginning of time. In fact, what you got is a well-known documented medical condition. They even got a scientific name for it.

YOLANDE. What?

LENORA. They call it the "I just got married and it ain't what I thought it was gonna be" blues.

YOLANDE. That's not no medical condition.

LENORA. I swear. Saw it in a medical book.

YOLANDE. Don't nobody believe you.

LENORA. Medical book said that women, they expect to wake up the morning after they get married and hear harp music and see butterflies flying around the room and shit like that.

YOLANDE. I never heard of none of this you talking about.

LENORA. I know you, and I know you expected to wake up and see blue skies, butterflies, and hear string music.

YOLANDE. Ain't nobody said nothing about hearing no string music.

LENORA. But you did expect to see blue skies and butterflies, didn't ya?

YOLANDE. I expected to feel like a wife.

LENORA. But how do you feel?

YOLANDE. I feel exactly the way I felt before I got married.

LENORA. "I just got married and it ain't what I thought it was gonna be" blues.

YOLANDE. I feel like I made a mistake.

LENORA. What happened? Did that nigger beat you?

YOLANDE. Oh heavens no.

LENORA. Did he hit you?

YOLANDE. No.

LENORA. Did he threaten to hit you?

YOLANDE. No, Lenora.

LENORA. Did he embarrass you?

YOLANDE. No.

LENORA. I see. Did he try to get you to commit some sort of unnatural sex act on him?

YOLANDE. What?

LENORA. Uh-huh. I knew it.

YOLANDE. What're you talking about?

LENORA. You shouldn't be such a prude, girl. I know what men like and I know that men like it when women do things like that. They like the attention. If fact, I don't see anything unnatural about it. Especially when the man responds in kind.

YOLANDE. What do you mean, respond in kind?

LENORA. When they do it back to you, honey. I like the feel of a man's lips down there. His tongue. I like the warmth of his breath.

YOLANDE. What on earth are you talking about?

LENORA. I'm talking about using your mouth, girl. And I'm not talking about talking.

YOLANDE. Oh no.

LENORA. You ought to try it. You might like it. And who knows? He responds in kind, and maybe you could find them blue skies and butterflies you been looking for.

YOLANDE. That was not the problem, Lenora.

LENORA. Then what was the problem? How did it go on your wedding night?

YOLANDE. What do you mean, how did it go?

LENORA. You know what I mean. Was he happy? Did you satisfy him?

YOLANDE. That's none of your business.

LENORA. It's never been anything other than none of my business. Now tell me. How many times did you do it?

YOLANDE. I don't know.

LENORA. You lost count?

YOLANDE. It was a very long night.

LENORA. What about the very first time that you did it? Did it take him a real long time to get done or did he get done real quick and keep coming back for more?

YOLANDE. Why are you asking me so many questions?

LENORA. Why you being so defensive?

YOLANDE. My life is not on public display.

LENORA. Since when did I become the public?

YOLANDE. You are asking very personal questions.

LENORA. This is a very personal matter, Yolande. Somebody told me that he was going to Paris without you. Is that true?

YOLANDE. We decided to meet there around Christmas.

LENORA. Then who is he going to Paris with?

YOLANDE. He's not going with anybody.

LENORA. Then he's going alone.

YOLANDE. Not exactly.

LENORA. Either he's going alone or he's going with somebody, Yolande. It's got to be one or the other. Who is he going with?

YOLANDE. Harold Jackman.

LENORA. The best man from your wedding?

YOLANDE. I don't understand what any of this has got to do with the price of butter.

LENORA. All right, then forget it.

YOLANDE. What you mean by that?

LENORA. By what?

YOLANDE. "All right then forget it."

LENORA. It means "all right, then forget it."

YOLANDE. You not fooling nobody. I know what you thinking.

LENORA. Is that right?

YOLANDE. That's right.

LENORA. You now a mind reader on top of everything else?

YOLANDE. That little mind of yours is not that difficult to read.

LENORA. What you might be reading are your own thoughts, Yolande. You ever think of that? Some people see only what they wanna see, no matter what's standing right in front of them. Now I'm gonna ask you something. You can answer if you feel like it, but you know what? It really don't matter to me. But I'm only gonna ask you once. That night, after your wedding, did Countee make you his wife?

YOLANDE. He had some problems.

LENORA. What kind of problems?

YOLANDE. Man problems.

LENORA. What about the night after that?

YOLANDE. He needed time to rest.

LENORA. Rest? According to you, he wasn't doing nothing.

YOLANDE. He's been doing a lot of work.

LENORA. What kind of work?

YOLANDE. He's a poet, Lenora.

LENORA. I understand that. But you still ain't told me what kind of work he's doing that requires him to need time to rest.

YOLANDE. If we do it too much, it'll fatigue his brain and interfere with his work and the work he's doing is very important.

LENORA. Has this man even laid a hand on you yet?

YOLANDE. He's been under a lot of pressure.

LENORA. Ain't that much pressure in the world.

YOLANDE. What do you know about it?

LENORA. The man hasn't touched you yet. That's the reason you don't feel any different. And now he's ready to sail to Paris with the best man from your wedding.

YOLANDE. You think that maybe…

LENORA. You're not dumb, Yolande. If you're happy with this, it's not my place to tell you anything different. You the only person who can say what you see when you look at that man and can't nobody get inside of you and look out through your eyes. Just make sure that what you're looking at is something that's outside of you, Yolande. Just make sure that what you're looking at is not a reflection of the world that you've created inside of your own head.

Scene Four

YOLANDE and COUNTEE. COUNTEE is packing.

COUNTEE. Every time I think I'm done packing I find something else I think I ought to bring. So I open the trunk thinking I'm gonna add just one item. Next thing I know, the trunk is empty and everything that took me ten days to put into the trunk is spread out all over the room and I'm right back where I was when I started packing ten days ago. Think I ought to bring this seersucker?

YOLANDE. I think it's gonna be a lil too cool for seersucker.

COUNTEE. You're right.

YOLANDE. 'Course I am.

COUNTEE. Don't know what I'd do without you.

YOLANDE. Funny. I was just asking myself the same question.

COUNTEE. Everything all right?

YOLANDE. I wanna go with you.

COUNTEE. I know you do. And I want you to go with me.

YOLANDE. That's not what I mean.

COUNTEE. But we're gonna have to wait till December.

YOLANDE. I've changed my mind, Countee. I want to go with you now.

COUNTEE. That's not possible right now.

YOLANDE. Why isn't it possible?

COUNTEE. We don't have the money.

YOLANDE. We have enough.

COUNTEE. Not for you to travel first class.

YOLANDE. I don't care about traveling first class anymore. I'll travel second class or tourist class if I have to.

COUNTEE. You're willing to travel tourist class to Paris?

YOLANDE. I'll ride in steerage if that's what it takes. But
  when you sail, I wanna sail with you, Countee. I don't
  wanna stay here alone.

COUNTEE. What about your job?

YOLANDE. My job can wait.

COUNTEE. You told them you were going to start in Sep-
  tember.

YOLANDE. I know what I told them and I'll tell them
  something different. If they don't like it, they can hire
  somebody else, but I don't wanna stay here alone.

COUNTEE. Yolande, even if we agreed that we should
  travel together, and even if we both agreed to travel
  tourist class, and if we kept track of every single nickel
  that passed through our hands, we still would not have
  enough money.

YOLANDE. But there's enough for you to travel with Harold Jackman?

COUNTEE. Harold Jackman is making a considerable contribution towards the expenses.

YOLANDE. I will make a considerable contribution towards expenses.

COUNTEE. You don't have the money.

YOLANDE. I will get the money.

COUNTEE. From where?

YOLANDE. All you have to do is tell me how much we
  need.

COUNTEE. Your father?

YOLANDE. Don't worry about where the money comes
  from.

COUNTEE. Your father's already paid for our wedding and for our honeymoon.

YOLANDE. That's not your concern, Countee.

COUNTEE. I can't accept any more money from your father.

YOLANDE. That money is my money. The money is in my name, money my father set aside for me. All you have to do is tell me how much we're gonna need. I will get it.

COUNTEE. And what about Harold? What am I supposed to tell him?

YOLANDE. You tell him that there's been a change of plans. That you've decided to travel to Paris with your wife. That's what you tell him.

COUNTEE. What's the matter with you?

YOLANDE. I wanna be on that boat with you when you leave for Paris.

COUNTEE. Yolande, I need to spend some time with Harold.

YOLANDE. Then have lunch with him before we sail.

COUNTEE. It has to be more than just an hour or two.

YOLANDE. Then invite him along. Is that what you want? Invite him along. The three of us. We can travel together.

COUNTEE. Yolande, I need to spend this time with Harold alone.

YOLANDE. What're you talking about?

COUNTEE. These past few months have been very difficult for me.

YOLANDE. It's been very difficult for the both of us.

COUNTEE. Yolande, it's important for you to understand that the time will always come when I will need to spend time with Harold alone.

YOLANDE. Explain this to me.

COUNTEE. He is a close and dear friend and as a close and dear friend, there are things that he and I need to talk about.

YOLANDE. What things?

COUNTEE. Private things.

YOLANDE. Things you can't discuss with me?

COUNTEE. Things that I may be able to discuss with you one day but not this day.

YOLANDE. How about tomorrow?

COUNTEE. Why are you doing this?

YOLANDE. I thought I was your wife.

COUNTEE. You are my wife.

YOLANDE. Then why haven't you made me your wife?

COUNTEE. This again.

YOLANDE. Why haven't you touched me?

COUNTEE. We've been over this, Yolande.

YOLANDE. Have we?

COUNTEE. Yes, we have.

YOLANDE. I'm having a bit of trouble remembering that particular conversation. Refresh me.

COUNTEE. I thought we had found pleasures in this world that were greater than those of carnal pleasure.

YOLANDE. You talking about a peck on the cheek? Is that what you're talking about? Holding hands and reciting poetry? Is this your pleasure greater than carnal pleasure?

COUNTEE. Now you're mocking me.

YOLANDE. What kind of pleasure do you have with Harold? Is it also a pleasure greater than carnal pleasure?

COUNTEE. Harold is my confidant.

YOLANDE. Lenora is my confidant but I don't have the need to spend private time alone with her.

COUNTEE. Maybe you should try it. Who knows? You might find that you like it.

YOLANDE. What are you saying to me?

COUNTEE. I made it clear to you before we were married that I had no intentions of giving up my relationship with my friend Harold. I even encouraged you to keep your relationship with your friend Jimmy. Nobody told you to go out and cut him off at the knees.

YOLANDE. Jimmy and I were a lot more than just friends.

COUNTEE. Oh really. Guess what. Harold and I are a lot more than just friends.

YOLANDE. Jimmy wanted to have relations with me.

COUNTEE. Are you sure you want to continue to draw parallels?

YOLANDE. You had relations with Harold Jackman?

COUNTEE. You and I have been chosen, Yolande.

YOLANDE. Answer my question.

COUNTEE. We have a job to do. We have to figure out a way to do that job without laying out our entrails for the vultures to eat. That means we have to be smart, we have to be vigilant, and we have to keep certain things in our lives private.

YOLANDE. You lied to me.

COUNTEE. I never lied.

YOLANDE. What else don't I know about you?

COUNTEE. You know everything.

YOLANDE. What about your mother?

COUNTEE. My mother?

YOLANDE. Where is she? You told me she died in child-birth.

COUNTEE. She did.

YOLANDE. Where is she, Countee?

COUNTEE. She lives on a farm in eastern Kentucky.

YOLANDE. Jesus, no. I'm not staying married to you.

COUNTEE. Because I lied about my mother?

YOLANDE. Because I don't know who you are.

COUNTEE. You know everything about me, Yolande.

YOLANDE. No.

COUNTEE. Look at me. I haven't changed. I swore to you that I would not change. I am the same man who made you laugh at dinner, the man with whom you danced until two a.m. almost every night. I am the man who stood with you at the altar. The man who put his trust in you after you swore to keep that trust.

YOLANDE. And now you're the man who's about to sail to Paris with his best friend instead of me. No, Countee. I'm not staying married to you.

COUNTEE. Is that what this is about? You want to go to Paris with me?

YOLANDE. Not anymore.

COUNTEE. Fine. It's done. I'll see Harold later today. I'll explain the situation to him.

YOLANDE. Nothing to explain.

COUNTEE. Yolande, listen. I didn't understand how important this was to you. Now that I understand, I can make adjustments.

YOLANDE. Don't bother. I don't want to fatigue your brain and interfere with your work.

COUNTEE. Please don't mock me.

YOLANDE. You mock me.

COUNTEE. But I can make amends. I will speak with Harold.

YOLANDE. I don't want you to speak with him. In fact, I don't even want my name falling from your lips.

COUNTEE. He can stay here in New York and you and I will sail to Paris together.

YOLANDE. I don't wanna go to Paris. Not with you. Not now.

COUNTEE. Why are you doing this to me? We talked about this, Yolande. We swore we would try to keep things as they were.

YOLANDE. What do you want? You want to freeze me in time? You want my yesterday to be like my today and my today to be like my tomorrow? No, I'm not gonna live like that. Not when it began with a lie.

Scene Five

Rehearsal hall. JIMMY does a soft-shoe as he softly sings. LENORA and YOLANDE watch him. LENORA takes notes with a pad and pencil.

JIMMY. I like cake and no mistake
        But baby if you insist
        I'll cut out cake
        Just for your sake
        Baby, come on and knock me a kiss.

        I like pie I hope to die
        Just get a load of this

When you get high
Doggone the pie
Baby, come on and knock me a kiss.

When you press your lips to mine
'Twas then I understood
They taste like candy
Brandy and wine
Peaches, bananas and everything good.

I love jam and no flimflam
Scratch that off my list
This ain't no jam
The jam can scram
Baby, come on and knock me a kiss.

YOLANDE. Working on a new routine?

JIMMY. You could say that. *(To LENORA.)* You get all that down?

LENORA. Got it.

JIMMY. Then I'm done. Would you get my stuff for me?

(LENORA exits.)

YOLANDE. You finished the song.

JIMMY. Finished it a long time ago.

YOLANDE. Sounds good. I heard it for the first time last night. Heard the whole thing. That was something, seeing your name up in lights on the marque at the Cotton Club. I was standing outside. Wish I could have come in, but you know, no colored allowed. Stood outside during the whole show. Baby, you were swanging. I got

a chance to peek in every now and then and saw what
you did with the orchestra. That was something, the way
you got them all moving together. Looked good, too.
People loved it. And the place was packed. I did get a
chance to come inside after you were done playing. I
caught a glimpse of you right before you went backstage
but I doubt if you saw me.

JIMMY. I saw you.

YOLANDE. I waited around for you.

JIMMY. I was busy.

YOLANDE. I figured that out after they told me you had
left.

JIMMY. Band business.

YOLANDE. Look, Jimmy, I'm sorry about the way things
happened.

JIMMY. Nothing to be sorry about. You made a choice.
People do that in life. They make choices. I just wish I
would've known that a choice was being made, that's
all. I got this feeling that if I would've known, maybe I
could've said something or done something. Who
knows? Maybe I would've carried that damn silver-tipped walking stick. But then again, maybe not.
But, we'll never know now, will we?

YOLANDE. Funny how things work out, huh?

JIMMY. Yeah, funny.

YOLANDE. I'm still the same person I was before.

JIMMY. No, Yolande. You are many years older than the
young girl you were a few months ago. You have aged.
You have turned into a woman. I can see it in the way
you walk, in the way you try to smile. No, you're nothing like the way you were a few months ago.

YOLANDE. You don't understand what I'm saying. You see, Countee, that's my husband...

JIMMY. I know the nigger's name.

YOLANDE. Countee and I have what I consider to be a modern marriage. We have decided not to adhere to convention.

JIMMY. You mean that you're keeping your apartment in Baltimore and that he's keeping his place in New York? Is that what you're talking about? That you're gonna see each other once or twice a week or maybe once or twice a month? Is this your idea of a modern marriage?

YOLANDE. I admit it, Jimmy. I made a mistake. But I'm the same person, Jimmy, I'm the exact same person I was before. Nothing's changed. I made a very stupid mistake but I can make it up to you, Jimmy. I can give you what you want.

JIMMY. I doubt that.

YOLANDE. But I can. You'll see. When you touch me, you'll see that I am the exact same person I was before. Only difference, I'm ready for you now, Jimmy. I'm ready to do all of those things that we talked about. And I want to do them with you again and again and again. I'm gonna keep my apartment in Baltimore. You can come and see me whenever you get ready. And I can come see you when I come to New York.

JIMMY. Sounds wonderful. Only problem is, you happen to be married.

YOLANDE. Doesn't matter.

JIMMY. Doesn't matter to who? To him? Why am I not surprised.

YOLANDE. I will go with you right now, Jimmy. Anywhere, I don't care. Back to your place. I don't care where it is or what it looks like. I will go with you and give you everything that I have to give, if you will take me and make me yours.

JIMMY. That's very nice, Yolande.

YOLANDE. I am offering to give you everything that you wanted.

JIMMY. Is that what you think I wanted? To lay up with you like a dog? To turn out the lights, take off my clothes and conduct some sort of business with you?

YOLANDE. Doesn't have to be like that, Jimmy.

JIMMY. I wanted all of you, Yolande. Not just the part that I can see and touch. I also wanted the part of you that used to get inside of me and stay with me long after you were gone. But you went and gave that part to somebody else. And now here you come offering me, what? The leftovers? Your carcass? I don't need you for that. There's a whole boatload of women out there who would give me that. If that's all I wanted, I would have gone to one of them a long time ago, 'cause they know how to do it, probably a lot better than you do, and they only charge a dollar.

(LENORA enters with a topcoat, scarf, white gloves and cane.)

JIMMY. I hope you find what you're looking for. I hope you find what you need. I wish you all the happiness in the world and I mean that, sincerely. *(To LENORA.)* You ready?

LENORA. How about I catch up with you?

JIMMY. No need to hurry. I'll see you when you get home. *(JIMMY kisses LENORA and exits.)*

YOLANDE. I see.

LENORA. He didn't tell you?

YOLANDE. I should have guessed. The way you would talk about him all the time. Talk about his hands, his arms, his chest...

LENORA. I know you're not upset about this.

YOLANDE. I gues you know what the men like.

LENORA. What's that supposed to mean?

YOLANDE. Did you use your mouth on him?

LENORA. He wanted somebody to.

YOLANDE. I'm sorry. I shouldn't have said that.

LENORA. Did you think that when you left, that the entire world would just stop turning? That everything would just freeze in time? Is that what you thought?

YOLANDE. I don't know what I thought.

LENORA. The world moves on, Yolande, with you or without you.

YOLANDE. You were right about Countee.

LENORA. I'm sorry.

YOLANDE. I don't know what to do. I don't want to stay married to him.

LENORA. You don't have to stay married to him.

YOLANDE. What am I supposed to do?

LENORA. Get a divorce.

YOLANDE. My father would die.

LENORA. Then don't get a divorce. Divorces are for people whose marriages have failed and your marriage didn't fail. According to you, you never had a marriage to begin with so you don't have to be divorced. Tell your father about Countee then have your marriage annulled.

YOLANDE. Do you know what that would look like? What people would think?

LENORA. It would probably look like he never made you his wife. What people would think would resemble the truth.

YOLANDE. The scandal that would cause.

LENORA. You have to stop thinking about others and start thinking about Yolande.

YOLANDE. I can't even imagine...

LENORA. Try to imagine. Imagine Yolande as being first and foremost. Not the poor, not the downtrodden, and certainly not your father. Yolande.

YOLANDE. That's a nice ring you have there. A diamond and two sapphires.

LENORA. This? Yeah, I uh...I...I...

YOLANDE. It's all right, Lenora. Does this mean you're getting married?

LENORA. No. He just gave it to me to wear. I only wear it 'cause I know it was yours.

YOLANDE. Can I ask you something?

LENORA. Sure.

YOLANDE. You ever...you know...with another woman?

LENORA. No. You?

YOLANDE. No. You ever think about trying? I mean, we are friends after all.

LENORA. We ain't never been that good of friends. What's the matter with you? That man's got you thinking all backwards and sideways. You better tell your daddy about him and get this over with so you can get on with your life and stop bothering me with all of this strange-ass behavior. You understand me, Yolande? Go and tell your daddy.

Scene Six

The Du Bois home. Early morning.

NINA. Yolande? Wake up, hon. You didn't sleep out here all night, did you?

YOLANDE. I must have.

NINA. You can catch the curvature of the spine by sleeping in chairs like that. You should sleep in the bed, honey. Nice, firm, sturdy bed.

YOLANDE. I know.

NINA. Countee's here looking for you. Says he hasn't seen you for a few days. Didn't you tell him you were gonna be here?

YOLANDE. I haven't told him anything.

NINA. Problems?

YOLANDE. I guess you could say that.

NINA. Countee really looks worried.

YOLANDE. He ought to be worried.

NINA. That's no way to be, Yolande. I'll let him know you're here.

YOLANDE. No, wait. Please. Don't tell him I'm here. Daddy home yet?

NINA. Came in late last night.

YOLANDE. Where is he?

NINA. He's in his room. What's going on, Yolande?

YOLANDE. Nothing.

NINA. You've been crying.

YOLANDE. Everything's fine, Mother.

NINA. What you want me to tell Countee?

YOLANDE. Countee can wait.

NINA. I have something that might cheer you up. A surprise. Actually, it's more like an early present. *(NINA presents a small package to YOLANDE. YOLANDE opens the package.)* I went to see Helen Keller speak the other day. You know who she is? She's that blind and deaf woman who learned how to talk by touching the lips and the throat of a speaker while the words the speaker spoke were being spelled out on the palm of her hand. Isn't that amazing? Anyway, I was on my way home from hearing her speak and I saw it in the window at Zimmerman's. It was so adorable, I'm sorry, I couldn't resist. *(In the package is a baby's jumper.)* It's for you. Well, actually not for you, it's for your baby, Yolande. I wanted to be the first one to give you something. I hope that wasn't selfish of me. I know I should've waited a bit. Waited at least until you were showing, but if you don't tell anybody, I won't.

YOLANDE. Mother, there is no baby.

NINA. Of course not. Not yet. But you just wait. In about seven months, you're gonna have the biggest surprise.

YOLANDE. No, Mother.

NINA. You may think you're ready, but believe me when I tell you, when that time comes, you'll find out that it's nothing like you thought it was gonna be.

YOLANDE. Seven, eight, nine, ten months, a year. It doesn't matter. There will be no baby.

NINA. Why not?

YOLANDE. I lost it. I lost the baby.

NINA. Oh my sweetness. It's happening. All over again. Just like before. Just like Burghardt.

YOLANDE. No, Mother.

NINA. I told your father, I didn't want to move to Atlanta. I made it clear to him, Yolande. There were no hospitals for Negroes. And everything might have been fine if Burghardt hadn't gotten sick. The nurse at the desk, she wouldn't admit Burghardt. They wouldn't even look at him. All he needed was a little medicine, and they had the medicine in ample supply behind those huge stone walls. It took us the rest of the night and most of the morning to find one of the three Negro doctors on the other side of town who would treat Burghardt but by then it was too late. Your father said that it was not his fault, but he moved us to that godforsaken place, for his work, he said. And that's the reason Burghardt is dead. He never even had a chance to live. Your father, who loved his son dearly, placed his son on the altar and sacrificed him without giving it a second thought. And now you tell me that you've lost your child and I can't help but to wonder, what did your father do this time.

YOLANDE. He didn't do anything, Mother.

NINA. How did you lose the baby?

YOLANDE. I just lost it. Daddy didn't have anything to do with me losing it, Mother.

NINA. Okay, Yolande. I'm gonna believe you. I just hope what I'm gonna believe is the truth.

(COUNTEE enters.)

COUNTEE. Excuse me.

NINA. I thought she might have been in here. I guess I was right. I'll get rid of all of this paper. *(She gathers up the wrapping paper and exits.)*

COUNTEE. I had been looking for you.

YOLANDE. I know.

COUNTEE. I spoke with Harold…

YOLANDE. I don't wanna hear about Harold.

COUNTEE. Look, Yolande…

YOLANDE. It's over. I'm gonna tell my father.

COUNTEE. Tell him what?

YOLANDE. Everything. I'm sorry, but I have to. I'm gonna have our marriage annulled.

COUNTEE. Yolande, please explain to me what happened between us to make you feel as if you had to consider resorting to this.

YOLANDE. It all began with a lie, Countee.

COUNTEE. But I love you, Yolande. I will do anything. All you have to do is tell me what you want. Just tell me what you want me to do and I will do it.

YOLANDE. I want you to make me your wife.

COUNTEE. Okay. Done.

YOLANDE. Now. I want you to do it now.

COUNTEE. You mean…

YOLANDE. Right here and now. We can go on the floor. On the desk. In the chair. Doesn't matter. The choice is yours.

COUNTEE. Are you serious?

YOLANDE. You said you would do anything.

COUNTEE. But…your mother…

YOLANDE. Did you mean it? Or was that just another lie?

(She starts to unbutton his shirt. He tries to touch her. She tries to touch him. They pick up a little momentum. Suddenly, COUNTEE stops.)

COUNTEE. I can't do this.

YOLANDE. Do you want me to help you?
COUNTEE. Help me?
YOLANDE. I could kiss you. I could use my mouth.
COUNTEE. What do you think I am?

(COUNTEE breaks away from YOLANDE and fumbles to restore his buttons as WILL enters.)

WILL. Good. You both are here. I have something for you. You've received letters of congratulations from various people and I've taken the liberty to answer the important letters with notes of thanks, especially to Judge Julian Mack. *(He hands a letter to COUNTEE.)* All you have to do is sign the letter and I'll have my secretary post it. *(He offers COUNTEE a pen which COUNTEE takes to sign the letter.)* I will have the other letters ready for you to sign later today. *(COUNTEE offers the letter to YOLANDE. YOLANDE takes it and reads it. COUNTEE offers her the pen.)* No need to read it. It's simple enough. "Thank you for your note of congratulations. With your blessing, our marriage will be one of happiness and of bliss."
YOLANDE. And you want me to sign it?
WILL. It's a thank-you note, Yolande.
YOLANDE. I'm not signing this.
WILL. Why not?
YOLANDE. "Our marriage will be one of happiness and of bliss"?
WILL. What's the problem?
YOLANDE. My marriage is not one of happiness, Daddy. It is not one of bliss.

WILL. I understand, you're having problems. Problems are to be expected, Ouchie. Usually the problem stems from the fact that we, as a nation, are not forthright when it comes to the subject of relations. As a result, the man quite innocently assumes that his wife will enjoy relations as much as he does which is usually not the case. Girls are usually extremely sensitive in their organs. Therefore, that which gives the husband pleasure may, for the girl, be exquisite physical torture.

YOLANDE. What are you talking about?

WILL. I'm talking about problems which come with marriage, Yolande. It was your mother's responsibility to explain these things to you but she has clearly, once again, failed her responsibility.

YOLANDE. That's not the problem, Daddy.

WILL. Countee, please. I'm gonna ask you for your patience in this matter.

YOLANDE. Why are you asking him for his patience? What about me? What about my patience?

WILL. Daughter, please.

YOLANDE. Daughter?

WILL. Countee? Would you excuse us for a moment?

YOLANDE. What're you talking about? Why are you asking him for his patience?

(COUNTEE exits.)

WILL. Yolande, you are no longer a little girl. You are a woman and you have been entrusted with a great and exciting responsibility. Stop feeling sorry for yourself and concentrate on your main duty and that is of being of assistance to Countee so that he may complete a year's work to which the world will listen.

YOLANDE. He's never touched me, Daddy. He's never touched me, he doesn't kiss me.

WILL. What do you think marriage is? You expect to continue to carry on like a couple of school children?

YOLANDE. We never carried on in the first place. Countee doesn't carry on. Not with me, he doesn't. With Harold Jackman, maybe, but not with me.

WILL. What are you saying?

YOLANDE. He is abnormal, Daddy.

WILL. He is carrying a great burden upon his shoulders.

YOLANDE. Sexually. He is sexually abnormal.

WILL. Most women believe that most men are sexually abnormal. But he's a man, Yolande. He has an appetite. This is perfectly normal.

YOLANDE. If he has an appetite, it's not for me, or for any other woman. Countee has an appetite for other men.

WILL. Where did you hear such a vicious and malicious lie?

YOLANDE. From Countee. He told me himself.

WILL. I refuse to believe it.

YOLANDE. Ask him yourself. He'll probably tell you.

WILL. Yolande, if this is true, if he actually confessed this to you, then you have no right to repeat it to me or to anyone else. Your husband spoke to you in confidence, Yolande. It is imperative that you keep that confidence.

YOLANDE. Didn't you even hear anything I just said?

WILL. Countee is doing work that will usher in a new way of thinking in this country. He is writing about love, about music, about the souls of black folks. His work will change the way America views the problem of race in this country and all you can think about is yourself? You've been spoiled, Yolande. And I admit, it's partially my fault for giving you everything you've ever wanted. As a result, you developed no sense of responsibility.

YOLANDE. Is that what I am? One of your failed projects?

WILL. You are my daughter.

YOLANDE. Or maybe I'm another sacrificial lamb.

WILL. I love you deeply.

YOLANDE. Just like you loved Burghardt?

WILL. I love you both the same.

YOLANDE. Please don't tell me that, Daddy.

WILL. I don't love him any more.

YOLANDE. No.

WILL. I don't love you any less.

YOLANDE. Mother was wrong about you. She said you were a beast, but she was wrong. You're not the beast. You're feeding the beast. You're keeping it alive.

WILL. I am fighting it with every ounce of my existence.

YOLANDE. You are feeding it the flesh and the bones of your own children.

WILL. I have dedicated my life to the end of racism. But I'm only one man, Yolande. I cannot slay it alone. I need your help.

YOLANDE. I'm not a soldier. I'm not gonna give my life for your cause.

WILL. It's your cause as well.

YOLANDE. No.

WILL. You want to teach high school? You want to help the downtrodden and the less fortunate? If you were truly committed to joining the struggle you would forget about "i before e except after c" and embrace your real responsibility, and that is of helping a great poet to become even greater so that we may finally prove to the entire world that the Negro race has pride, power, potential and glory. Go to him, Yolande. Be of assistance to him. Reach up and remove a stone from the wall of segregation and help me push it over onto this rampaging beast so that we may all one day live in peace. Sign the note. I'll post it the first thing in the morning.

YOLANDE *(takes the note)*. You want the note signed? *(She crumples the note and tosses it to the floor.)* You sign it. I've already been complicit in too many lies.

(WILL exits as COUNTEE enters.)

COUNTEE. You tell him?

YOLANDE. I told him.

COUNTEE. Everything? And what did he say?

YOLANDE. I don't think he understood. Or maybe he didn't care to understand.

COUNTEE. Yolande, please, I know that between the two of us, we can find happiness.

YOLANDE. The happiness you're offering me is not enough. I need more, Countee.

COUNTEE. What more?

YOLANDE. I need you to knock me a kiss.

COUNTEE. What?

YOLANDE. I told you that you could trust me and I plan to keep that trust but I will not stay married to you. I'm gonna sue you for a divorce, Countee. And you will give me that divorce. And if you make any trouble for me or if you say anything unkind about me, I will take that trust and I will split it open and lay it out on the table for the entire world to feast upon. You understand me?

COUNTEE. I understand.

YOLANDE. Have a good time in Paris. Give Harold Jackman my best.

(COUNTEE puts his index finger to his lips, then moves to put it to her. She stops him. He exits as NINA enters.)

NINA. Countee's gone?

YOLANDE. He's gone.

NINA *(picks up the baby jumper).* You mind if I keep this? I would like to put it with Burghardt's things as a reminder. Did I tell you about Helen Keller? She was stricken with an illness that left her blind and deaf when she was nineteen months old. I thought what had happened to her must have been the absolute worst calamity that could ever befall a person. I thought that not being able to hear another human voice, not being able to see another human face must be a fate worse than death. I now realize that there are worse fates in this world. You see, I have eyes that appear to function as eyes, but they see nothing but darkness. And I have ears and I can hear sounds but the only sounds I hear are grunts, moans, whimpers and howls. And while a woman who was born deaf and blind was able to learn to speak by touching the lips and the throat of a speaker, I am unable to touch or to be touched and therefore, I will never learn to speak. I open my mouth to speak but nothing comes out. I flail my arms in darkness and come in contact with nothing. Do you know what that's like? To have all of your senses removed? Not being able to see? To hear?

To smell? To touch? To taste? I am old, Yolande. My desire dull. My feelings have been crusted over with memories of what could have been. But here I am talking about me again and you would think that I would know by now that you don't want to hear about me. I think I'll have a bit of tea, that's what I think I'll do. Miss Otis says that the green tea helps, and you know what? I think she's right. *(NINA moves to exit.)*

YOLANDE. May I have a bit as well?

NINA. Of tea? You want to have a bit of tea with me?

YOLANDE. Yes. I would like to have a bit of tea with you, Mother.

NINA. Okay. But you must be patient with me, Yolande. It may take a while for me to find another cup.

(Lights fade.)

End of Play

DIRECTOR'S NOTES

DIRECTOR'S NOTES